TEAM
MINISTRY

A WORKBOOK FOR GETTING THINGS DONE

Stephen L. Schey
Walt Kallestad

Abingdon Press
Nashville

oversized 253.1
KT-431-845
20346

CONTENTS

**TEAM MINISTRY:
A WORKBOOK
FOR GETTING
THINGS DONE**

Copyright © 1996 by
Abingdon Press

All rights reserved
No part of this work may be
reproduced or transmitted in
any form or by any means,
electronic or mechanical,
including photocopying and
recording, or by any information storage or retrieval
system, except as may be
expressly permitted by the
1976 Copyright Act or in
writing from the publisher.
Requests for permission
should be addressed to
Abingdon Press, P.O. Box
801, 201 Eighth Avenue
South, Nashville, TN 37202-
0801.

This book is printed on recy-
cled, acid-free paper.

ISBN 0-687-01719-X

Scripture quotations are
from the New Revised
Standard Version Bible,
copyright © 1989, by the
Division of Christian
Education of the National
Council of the Churches of
Christ in the United States of
America.

96 97 98 99 00 01 02 03 04
05—10 9 8 7 6 5 4 3 2 1

MANUFACTURED IN THE
UNITED STATES OF AMERICA

INTRODUCTION

BUILDING QUALITY MINISTRY TEAMS IN YOUR CHURCH

Committed pastors and congregations desire to develop the best staff and volunteer organization possible. With the resources God and the members provide, when the needs for ministry have been clearly identified, the challenge is to organize and equip everyone for preaching the Word, administering the sacraments, and meeting the needs. This requires building quality ministry teams in your church!

Often a pastor ends up in a congregation that has long ago selected its staff and volunteer organization. Thus the pastor has little voice in the selection process. If one has the advantage of selecting the team, where does one start?

This workbook presents perhaps the ideal situation. It carefully outlines in a logical sequence the order in which a congregation might seek to build the most effective, efficient ministry team of staff and volunteers. We recognize that such an ideal situation is rarely found. Even congregations in which many of the points are mastered, peri-

ods of change in people, mission, or other situations may cause them to lose ground in certain areas. They will then need to refocus and gain back what they have lost.

We also recognize that a pastor will rarely find the opportunity to start from "ground zero" in building a ministry team. Often the culture of the congregation is firmly established and resistant to change. The pastor will be required to assess the climate for any of these points and start where success is most likely. Success in one area can often lead to success in another.

The story of creating this workbook began with building the staff and volunteers at Community Church of Joy. As in all stories, we continually go through transitions, and the ideal is yet to unfold. We hope the illustrations and stories developed in this environment may be of help to you as you make the critical application to your own congregation.

You may recognize terms and ideas that were presented by the authors in *Total Quality Ministry* (Augsburg Fortress, 1994). That book presents a translation of the principles of total quality management to the Christian church. It also discusses the overall philosophy of quality in congregations. Ministry teams, the focus of this workbook, are one part of the overall congregational quality process.

One of the critical principles of *Total Quality Ministry* is the emphasis on the shared vision of the congregation. Chapter 1 of this book begins laying this foundation for any team that serves in your church. How does a congregation determine its mission and vision? How is shared vision (which is so strongly promoted in the secular business community) created in a congregation?

With the mission and vision clearly understood and articulated, the congregation is ready for changes in organizational structure. This allows the shared mission and vision to be accomplished. Chapter 2 suggests an organizational structure that empowers staff and volunteers to use their gifts and abilities in ministry.

You will carefully consider the people you hire and place in key volunteer positions. Chapter 3 identifies the process of finding the right people so that your ministry can soar.

Once you have hired and appointed the key people, provide them the best atmosphere possible in which to work. Encourage them to use their gifts and abilities in creative ways to solve the ministry problems. Provide new ideas for meeting the ministry needs of people. Chapter 4 presents the environment desired for effective team ministry.

At a training conference we attended in Phoenix in 1995, Zig Ziglar observed that there is one thing worse than training an employee and losing him or her to another company: that is, not to train the employee and then keep him or her. It would be futile to expend the energy to find the best people possible and to create an environment where employees and volunteers can excel if you were unable to retain these employees and key volunteers. Chapter 5 provides suggestions on keeping these teammates active and involved in your ministry and not losing them to another.

The buzzword in business today is "teams." Corporations find that forming teams of people provides opportunities for synergism to create fantastic products. In like manner, teams within the congregation provide opportunities to solve problems and create new ministry ideas that transcend what the typical Lone Ranger can accomplish. Chapter 6 discusses team formation in the congregation.

Recognition and reward systems are also vitally important in relating to staff and volunteers. Chapter 7 involves finding ways to honor exceptional performance without creating competition. It suggests a new way to look at performance appraisals and how to involve team workers in their own evaluation system.

The creation of quality ministry teams may be a lengthy, intensified process. Being alert and aware of your goal to accomplish this can assist you in each of the hundreds of decisions you will make in the coming years. Knowing the objective makes it easier to take the crucial steps to putting the winning team together.

In many communities there is a familiar proverb: "If you don't know where you are going, any road will lead you there." Why wander around without a vision? If you do know where you are going, you have the opportunity to choose the road to lead you there. When you get on that road, ministry teams may be the most effective way to travel.

CHAPTER 1

THE STARTING POINT IS VISION

Steve takes his sons, Mike and Andrew, to a preseason baseball game at the Peoria Sports Complex. The California Angels are pitted against the San Diego Padres. Prior to the game there is utter chaos in the stands. Vendors are shouting over their beer and peanuts; friends are calling to others who have already found their seats; people are getting comfortable; players on the field are acknowledging the shouts of fans. Suddenly, the public address system announces the national anthem.

Slowly the chaos subsides as people stand, search for the flag, and finally focus on it. For the next few minutes, the entire stadium is unified. Singing or listening respectfully to the national anthem at baseball games is more than token patriotism, though it was no doubt sobering during the World Wars

as various team members were conscripted to serve and die for the liberty of other countries. The pledge is a centering act for the teams and the spectators, who are reminded that there is more to life than the game at hand.

From this act in baseball we observe that the starting point in building and maintaining a quality ministry team is creating a sharp focus that helps the team recall why they are part of a larger drama in ministry. This focus takes a group of people from concentrating on each person's individual interests, goals, desires, and passions to concentrating on the ministry's interests, goals, desires, and passions. This focus is created through the development of a *mision* and a *vision.*

MISSION

Why Create a Mission Statement?
The world is not the same as it once was. This is obvious, and it is always true, but many in the church do not want to believe it. Loren Mead's book *The Once and Future Church* describes a great history of paradigm shifts in the Christian community since the resurrection of Christ. Mead says that the early church lived under the "apostolic paradigm." Christians saw it as their responsibility to witness to others. Their mission field was right outside the front door of their church.[1]

When Constantine was converted to Christianity, the paradigm shifted to the "Christendom paradigm." Eventually, the church and the state became one. To be born into the Empire meant that one was born a Christian. Everyone was assumed to be Christian, so in terms of mission there was no need to witness to anyone about the good news in Jesus Christ. The mission field was in a faraway land, and witnessing was pursued by mission professionals who were trained by the church. Parishes were established geographically and ethnically, and since every parish was culturally conformed, being born into a family also determined the parish to which a person belonged.

Even after the Reformation, which perpetuated Christendom in alliance with European nation-states, it made sense for the church headquarters to train the professionals in mission. Churches were not involved in this training, other than through financial support, since they were organized to care for the flock in their parish. They were to preach the Word and administer the sacraments and be faithful to the traditions of the church. Every denominational church supposedly was the same, such that all Methodists in one geographic area belonged to the Methodist church there, all Lutherans belonged to the Lutheran church there, all Catholics belonged to their Catholic church. It was assumed during periods of population growth, particularly before the automobile

1. Loren Mead, *The Once and Future Church* (Washington, D.C.: Alban Institute, 1991).

allowed rapid transit, that all persons belonged to a church, and therefore telling the story of the faith with others remained a work for professionals in faraway places.

It is now common knowledge that we are in the "time between paradigms." Some theologians call it the "post-Christendom paradigm." It is no longer true that everyone around us is a Christian. It is not true that being born in the United States or in any other country automatically makes one a Christian. We are in a culture where more and more people are not Christian, and once again we are being called upon to witness to our story and share our faith with others. Once again the mission fields are directly outside our church doors.

Some of us can remember Sundays as days of relaxation and rest. There were few if any businesses open, and the commandment to "remember the sabbath day, and keep it holy" made sense to the rulers in our communities. Today, Sunday is increasingly like any other day. Do people today even understand a sabbath?

Identify other cultural changes in your community that show the changing of the paradigm to a "post-Christendom paradigm."

_____

_____

_____

_____

_____

Many church leaders today recognize that their mission is outside their church door. They recognize that preaching the Word, administering the sacraments, and being faithful to church traditions is not enough to keep the story of their faith from dying out. These ordained acts of religious professionals are insufficient for reaching the unchurched, keeping members in church, and reversing declines. Where once the denominational headquarters was able to identify the mission fields and prepare for mission, today the headquarters cannot understand the individual mission fields in every location. While trying to be faithful to their headquarters and still recognizing the diversity and unique nature of the individual mission fields, many church leaders are in a quandary over what to do.

Because the headquarters cannot understand every mission field, it is necessary that each church understand its own mission field. That is the purpose of the congregation's mission and its mission statement.

WHAT IS THE MISSION STATEMENT?

"**E**veryone has a wonderful plan for my life!" said a young pastor on his first call. Between the hospital visits, confirmation classes, Bible studies, sermon preparations, home visits, committee meetings, counseling appointments, meetings with city officials, curriculum meetings, and everything else, he had little time left for individual prayer, personal enrichment and training, and thinking about the future. It is much better to ask the question, "What plans does God have for my life?"

Have you not heard that I determined it long ago? I planned from days of old what now I bring to pass.

—Isaiah 37:26a

While we may be very busy doing God's work, we need to be sure we are doing what the Lord wants done. The question of effectiveness (doing the right thing) is as important as that of efficiency (doing it well). We could easily be doing the wrong things but doing them well. God has plans for us. We need to discern what they are.

What has God called us to do as the Lord's congregation?

The answer to this question defines our *mission*.

But before we can begin to address this question, we have a more personal question:

What has God called me to do?

MY PERSONAL MISSION

If God's call in your life is very evident to you, write the answer to this question here. **What has God called me to do?**

_____

_____

_____

_____

_____

_____

If the answer is not that clear, or it has been some time since you have thought about it, now would be a good time to consider this question anew.

This process begins with prayer. Ask God this question. Seek the Lord's will in your life. Seek God's call. God has promised to answer.

"Ask, and it will be given you; search, and you will find; knock, and the door will be opened for you."

—Matthew 7:7

As you seek God's will in prayer, write the answers here.

_____

_____

_____

_____

_____

What do you do that gives you special energy and drive?

_____

_____

_____

_____

_____

Next, identify your **SHAPE!**

Spiritual gifts. Identify your spiritual gifts below. If you have not taken a spiritual gifts survey recently, do so now. (See appendix A for a spiritual gifts survey.)

It is out of the abundance of the heart that the mouth speaks.

—*Luke 6:45b*

Now concerning spiritual gifts, brothers and sisters, I do not want you to be uninformed.

—*1 Corinthians 12:1*

Abilities. Consider your activities over the past five years. What activities have you done and continue to do well?

My Spiritual Gifts are:

1. _____

2. _____

3. _____

4. _____

_____

_____

_____

_____

What activities have you not done so well?

_____

Heart. Where is your heart in the *doing* of your ministry? What are your special interests?

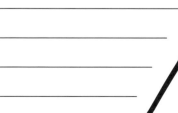

P *Passion.* What are the driving passions in your life? What motivates you for action beyond what you might consider reasonable? If resources were not an issue, what would be your dream?

_____

_____

_____

_____

_____

Therefore I have uttered what I did not understand, things too wonderful for me, which I did not know.

—Job 42:3

Now look over your **SHAPE**. Pray over your **SHAPE**. You should be able to discover your own call and mission in life. What has God called you to do? If you didn't answer the question before, answer it now.

CONGREGATIONAL MISSION

The congregation needs to determine its mission.

What has God called this congregation to do?

As before, the first step is to pray. Seek first God's inspiration and the revelation of the Lord's purpose in this congregation. Pray for the inspiration of key, mature leaders. Pray for your process. Pray for the acceptance by the congregation.

E *Experiences.* As God directs and leads our personal and spiritual growth, God provides experiences for us from which we can learn much. Identify some of the more vivid experiences (including painful ones) of your life.

1. _____

_____

2. _____

_____

3. _____

_____

4. _____

_____

The mission will not be determined by a committee that is appointed by the governing board. It will be sought by mature Christian leaders who truly seek God's will above their own interests. Select a few individuals to take a retreat with the pastor to seek God's will in earnest prayer and discussion. This process may not be quick. Ask the tough questions.

Contextualize your mission. Ensure that what you have determined makes sense in your location. Is this mission meeting the needs of God's people in your community? Does it match the overall **SHAPE** of the congregation?

Announcing

Next comes the promotion of the mission. Before announcing that you have discovered the mission, discuss it with many key leaders. Conduct a positive public relations campaign to gain support. You will eventually need to gain the support and endorsement of the governing board. Win them over to this mission. Ask them to prayerfully consider this mission. Do they see a different mission? Do they have other insight and ideas that should be considered?

This may be a very challenging time. *A mission may mean change.* Something new is happening. Things will be different. In later chapters we will discuss *change* and its management within teams in greater detail. Your personal leadership and influence will be important as you promote this mission.

Next comes the real promotion! A mission is of no value if it isn't known and practiced. It is important to summarize the mission into a short statement which can be easily memorized. This provides greater opportunity for it to be thought about and used. Find ways to publicly promote the mission. Preach about it, place it on banners, quote it in your worship bulletins, identify it on meeting agendas, require the staff, governing board, and key volunteers to memorize it.

FOR CLARITY, THE MISSION STATEMENT SHOULD BE

1. Biblical: To have the best potluck dinners may be a desirable goal for one of the teams, but it won't inspire many in the congregation. God's purpose for your congregation should be discernible in or consistent with the Scriptures.

2. Directed at a target: Who benefits from this ministry's existence? For whom is the mission targeted?

3. Results-oriented: What is it that we seek to accomplish? What is the desired outcome?

4. Purposeful: What are we doing? Why are we in existence? What do we do to accomplish our desired results?

"The Son of Man came to seek out and to save the lost."

—*Luke 19:10*

What an incredible mission statement! Jesus certainly had a mission and knew it exceedingly well. He never lost sight of his mission. His mission was central to everything he did, including his journey to the cross.

If you have an existing mission statement, review it to make sure it truly is reflective of God's call in your life and in your congregation. If it has been some time since the mission was prepared, take time to go through the process again.

Your mission is one of the most important things you will determine in your ministry. Without a compelling mission, teamwork is likely to be misguided activity.

WRITING YOUR MISSION STATEMENT

Prepare to write the mission statement for your congregation. Here are some examples:

That all may know Jesus Christ and become responsible members of His church, we share His love with joy, inspired by the Holy Spirit.[2]

We exist to

praise God,

prepare ourselves for service,

provide love and care for one another,

and proclaim Christ to the world.[3]

TARGET

Identify your target. Jesus identified "the lost."

Some congregations identify "all who may know"—which is interpreted to mean that they are highly focused on the "unchurched."

Who is your target? Which group of people receive the greatest priority for your congregation? All people are important, but upon whom will your congregation place the greatest energy?

_____

_____

_____

_____

_____

_____

_____

_____

_____

2. From Community Church of Joy (Lutheran).

3. From Hope United Methodist Church, as cited in Norman Shawchuck, et al., *Marketing for Congregations: Choosing to Serve People More Effectively* (Nashville: Abingdon Press, 1992), 223.

RESULTS

Identify the results you desire.

Jesus said that he came to save.

The result desired at one church is to make Christ known to all and to help transform people into responsible members.

What results are you called to achieve? What is it that you seek to accomplish?

_____

_____

_____

_____

_____

_____

_____

PURPOSE

What is your purpose? How will you reach your target and get the results?

Jesus said that he came to seek the lost. His earthly life, described in the Gospels, shows him going to wherever he could find the lost.

A congregation that is driven by the mission of helping all to know Jesus Christ will have the purpose of sharing the love of Christ, with joy, as inspired by the Holy Spirit.

What is your purpose? Why does your congregation exist? What do you do to accomplish your desired results?

_____

_____

_____

_____

_____

_____

_____

Now condense these three statements (target, results, purpose) into one brief statement that can be memorized. You cannot state your entire theology in one sentence and will need to realize that the mission statement alone is not enough to inspire people. As you discuss this with leaders and preach about the mission, people will begin to understand what is meant by this one statement.

_____

_____

_____

_____

_____

_____

For each of the major steps identified in preparing the mission and mission statement, record the date on which it was completed.

The day I began to consider preparing or reviewing the mission of this congregation:

_____

The day I began to earnestly pray for God to reveal his mission to be done in my life and in my congregation, to raise up the team needed, and to prepare my congregation:

_____

The day I organized my team to seek God's mission in my congregation and we worked to develop the mission and mission statement:

_____

The day the governing board approved the mission statement and we began to announce and promote it to the entire congregation:

_____

The day I gave thanks for God's leading in my life and the life of my congregation:

_____

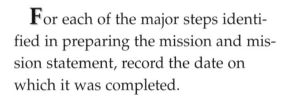

VISION

WHAT IS VISION?

Many books and dozens of speakers on the lecture circuit say that we must have vision. Leaders are visionary. Leaders create a shared vision. One characteristic that distinguishes between leaders and managers is vision. What does this mean?

Before you go any further, write your definition of *vision*:

_____

_____

_____

_____

_____

_____

_____

_____

_____

_____

_____

Merriam Webster's Collegiate Dictionary, tenth edition, defines *vision* as

In this dictionary definition for vision, the ability to perceive something physically (the third definition) isn't as important as the real power of *vision*.

Vision is an image of the present and future. Many times the image cannot be seen physically.

1. a: something seen in a dream, trance, or ecstasy; *esp:* supernatural appearance that conveys a revelation

b: an object of imagination

c: a manifestation to the senses of something immaterial

2. a: the act or power of imagination

b: (1) mode of seeing or conceiving
(2) unusual discernment or foresight

c: direct mystical awareness of the supernatural usu. in visible form

3. a: the act or power of seeing: sight

b: the special sense by which the qualities of an object... constituting its appearance are perceived and which is mediated by the eye

4. a: something seen

b: a lovely or charming sight

It is telling that those who lack vision often are looking only for the physical revelation or proof of concepts and ideas.

Vision pertains to concepts and feelings. Many parts of a vision cannot be expressed in absolutes. A vision involves quality, values, drive, effort, and atmosphere. A vision provides excitement as we look ahead. It focuses on *possibilities*, not problems. It is the spark that motivates action toward goals and objectives.

In this book, we define vision as consisting of six components:

V Values.

These are the beliefs and personal standards that drive decisions and actions. They help us to clarify gray areas. While a certain action may be legal, the visionary has values that compel the question, Is it moral? What is the *right* thing to do? It may not be the convenient thing. What is of greatest importance in your life?

Values include personal integrity, honesty, trustworthiness, truthfulness, and so on. Character counts. What is done in private will be revealed in public.

I Imagination.

Information is limited. Imagination is unlimited. Clearly God has an incredible imagination. Imagination is the instigator of inventions. Imagination leads you to investigate the unknown. Even if every material possession in the world is lost, with imagination we can rise up and rebuild.

S Servant's Heart.

We will discuss in the next chapter the importance of seeking servants when selecting persons to leadership positions for ministry teams. Jesus demonstrated his servant's heart and told us to do likewise. To overcome our relentless self-interest, we constantly need to be in service to others.

I Innovation.

Like imagination, innovation encourages new ideas. Imagination thinks of possibilities which may not currently exist. Innovation looks at what is and seeks to improve it. The last seven words of a dying church are, "We've never done it that way before." That is probably a good reason to try. Try new methods even when the old way seems to be working. Encourage staff and volunteers to think of new methods. Ask "Why?" frequently. Challenge everyone to question old ways and methods. Maybe they are the best, and this thinking will confirm that. If they are not the best, this thinking will encourage innovation.

O Optimistic Outlook.

Pessimistic dreams or projections will inspire no one. Be realistic and accurate with information, but seek what is positive. Be enthusiastic about what God has prepared. Seek the possibilities. Be aware of the problems but don't make them the focus. Seek solutions. Obstacles become opportunities. Put your best thinkers and problem solvers on the issues and don't settle for "can't."

Nurture.
Care for your people. Many cannot see the future. Most don't know how to see tomorrow. Some are not sure they will make it until tomorrow. As you care for your people, help them to make the transition from today's view to the future view. Help people through the chaos that happens anytime change is introduced. Without a vision, the people perish (or go to another parish).

VISION answers the question,

What has God called us to be as God's people?

For the congregation, **VISION** answers the question,

What has God called this congregation to be as God's congregation?

This question applies to both the present and the future.

VISION is a gift from God. For the congregation, that gift may be given to individuals or to a small group of people. Dreaming and *vision* do not come easily to everyone. Frequently, a *vision* granted to one will blossom into dreams in others, which will blossom into ideas for implementation in others.

> **For surely I know the plans I have for you, says the LORD, plans for your welfare and not for harm, to give you a future with hope.**
> —*Jeremiah 29:11*

As a gift, vision needs to be something we clearly ask God to provide. We spend time in prayer to determine God's plan for our future. We know God has a plan for us; God has said so.

The vision needs to be clearly communicated to the leaders of congregational teams, so that others can see and claim the vision and spark the dreaming and planning process.

HOW TO ENVISION GOD'S WILL

Envisioning God's will is perhaps easier said than done, since the vision may not be clear at first.

Confide in a small group of people you believe to be mature in their faith and truly seeking God's will for the future of the congregation. Tell them of your desire to envision the future. Seek time together in prayer and discussion over your future. Don't *plan* the future now; that comes later. Now you are simply dreaming and seeking God's desire.

There are several approaches to thinking about the future. Your thinking may be based upon specific goals, specific needs, or the big picture.

✔ SPECIFIC GOALS:

From what we understand of our congregational purpose and mission today, we expand our look to the future and set specific goals and targets for the future. A congregation that seeks the unchurched in a multicultural area might set a goal of developing a bilingual worship style.

What are your goals for the future? How do you see your mission changing or evolving in the next five years? How might your "target" be changing?

_____

_____

_____

_____

_____

_____

✔ SPECIFIC NEEDS:

What are the specific unmet needs or emerging needs of your community and your con-

stituents which you see as your responsibility to meet? What are the critical issues you face as a congregation? How will your future resolve these issues?

For example, a congregation that is rural but sees the urban expansion heading its way may need to address the coming population growth; a congregation faced with an aging constituency may need to think about how to minister for the current members while reaching out to new ones; a congregation that finds gang warfare is closer than it used to be may need to seek ways to teach peace. How will you address the issues facing your congregation?

_____

_____

_____

_____

_____

_____

✔ THE BIG PICTURE:

In this process, look to the future, test several major philosophical and directional assumptions about the congregation. Which path or scenario shall this congregation take?

A congregation faced with growth but limited space may consider establishing "daughter congregations," forming partnerships with adjacent businesses, relocating, or other alternatives. Each has specific effects on the future of the congregation.

In truth, as you envision the future, you will consider all these areas. Of highest priority, however, is a revelation that God might grant. As you are called in worship day by day to confess your shortcomings and repent of your sin, God's purpose often is to redirect your thoughts and efforts to align them with his will.

Just as you wrote down your mission statement, once you clearly understand the scope of the vision and the future, you must put it in writing. Prepare a one- or two-page summary of the vision you and your team have just prepared.

Share this vision statement with other trusted friends and key congregational leaders. Use your personal powers of persuasion and influence to gain support. Listen for feedback and be sensitive for new insights.

Be prepared for God to work in inspiring others with this vision. Some will begin to "see" what you see and absorb this vision as their own. Their imaginations will be ignited and some will begin to plan. Some will be driven to action to accomplish this vision. This will lead to strategic planning, which we will discuss further in chapter 3.

You will find that there is nothing more exciting than to have a dream for the future. People are excited about mission; but to begin to see the future and then plan and prepare for it ignites personal drive and enthusiasm.

In your congregation, this vision will pro-

vide unity among the leadership, staff, volunteers, and congregation. This vision will provide

direction
for all actions, plans, and decisions you need to make;

focus
for leadership, staff, volunteers, and members of the congregation;

information
on the plans and direction the congregation is taking;

motivation
to inspire the entire congregation;

enthusiasm
as it creates an attainable dream;

inspiration
as it calls forth the best in people and the congregation;

anticipation and expectation
of future events;

humility
as we realize our dependence on God to prepare the way to our future.

At times there is little happening at a baseball game. As the innings stretch on, the Angels are leading the Padres, but for the most part Steve and his sons eat their peanuts and talk. Suddenly, they hear a sound that everyone in the stadium recognizes. There is a distinctive "crack" as a bat hits a ball with tremendous power. They all know that the ball is well hit.

Those fans who are paying attention watch the ball rise in the air. Steve's youngest son is not watching. As the ball clears the infield and the crowd starts to rise in anticipation, Steve's son asks frantically, "Where is it? Where is it?"

Steve cannot describe where the ball is. He points to it as it levels out over the outfield. His son still cannot see it. It's hard to find the ball in midflight.

The crowd roars as the ball clears the center-field fence. Steve's son now sees where the people on the grass are scrambling to claim their prize. He is disappointed that he hasn't seen the whole flight.

Your congregation will react to your mission and vision in ways that remind you of this incident at the ball game. Some of your members will be paying attention and will catch the mission and vision, and they will be cheering in great enthusiasm as they see the "home run": the successes of ministry, the accomplishment of your mission, the transformation of lives through Jesus Christ.

Some of your colleagues will not be paying attention. The other cares of daily life, perhaps combined with lack of vision, will prevent them from finding the ball in flight. They won't see the ball clear the fence. They won't share in the excitement. Don't let them steal your dream. Don't let them dissuade you from the mission and vision God has granted. The home run counts even if they do not see it.

"Just so, I tell you, there will be more joy in heaven over one sinner who repents than over ninety-nine righteous persons who need no repentance."

—*Luke 15:7*

CHAPTER 11

ORGANIZING FOR EFFECTIVE TEAM MANAGEMENT

The young woman arrived at the church in great excitement about her call to be the youth director. With enthusiasm she relayed to the pastor her ideas for a big event to be her welcoming party but also to be a rallying point for youth who were lost to the program during the interim without a leader. She could see renewed excitement among the teens as she would begin to reestablish relationships that had been lost.

The pastor thought it was a great idea, but she could not make such a decision without the approval of the church council. The council would meet in two weeks, and she would ask permission.

During the meeting, the pastor relayed her excitement about the new youth director and suggested this big event to rally the youth. After deliberation, the council determined it was really a question that needed a recommendation by the youth committee. It was referred to that committee, which was to meet in three weeks.

At the youth committee meeting, there were several questions raised: How much money would it cost? Were the facilities sufficient? Who would be in charge—the Committee or the Director? This needed more time and thought. It was tabled until the next meeting, which was canceled due to inclement weather.

At the next monthly meeting, the questions were resolved, and it was recommended for approval at the next church council meeting, the following week.

The church council approved the action, but by this time ten weeks had elapsed. With the preparation time for the event, three months would have passed between the birth of the idea and its implementation. The opportunity for a fantastic beginning was lost. The youth director was already disappointed, discouraged, and had found other ways to begin to establish the relationships.

The building of high quality ministry teams in your church will require effective management and governance structures. The starting point is the mission and vision developed in chapter 1. In most cases, when the congregation understands, believes, and seeks to accomplish its mission and vision, it will seek ways to become more effective and efficient in its methods of governance and management. Without rejuvenation born of a fresh vision, attempts to change the governance structures will be met with apathy and regret.

In this chapter we will discover ways to evaluate the governance and management structures we put in place to see if they are effective in helping us to accomplish our ministry and mission. The organization of the management and governance teams are crucial to developing ministry teams who get things done.

GOVERNANCE

Congregations define their governing board in many different terms (many not too kind). Some are called church councils, some are called the session, some are called elders or trustees, some are called boards of directors. As we discuss governance, we will identify this governing body to be the group legally required and legally responsible for actions by nonprofit corporations: specifically churches, and we will call it the *governing board.* Substitute your own name for your congregation's governing body when you see this term.

Your congregation's organizing documents identify the specific responsibilities of the governing board. Find your articles of incorporation, your constitution, and your bylaws. These will identify the areas for which your governing board is legally responsible.

It is at this point that many congregations confuse governance and management. Although the governing board is *responsible* for the things listed, it is not necessarily true that the governing board needs to *do* them. The governing board sets certain policies, but the staff (paid and unpaid) ensures that the policies are followed. The governing board approves the budget (as does the congregation in many cases), but the staff manages the funds. The governing board establishes the plans to reach the vision, but the staff (paid and volunteer) takes the day-to-day action.

Is this the model in use in your congregation? In what ways is your structure different?

_____

_____

_____

_____

THE TRADITIONAL GOVERNANCE STRUCTURE

T H E   W O R K   G R O U P

Many denominations have established a form of governance that presupposes the Christendom paradigm. This style of governance is called the *work group.* In this style, the elected members of the governing board are also assigned specific duties in the management of the organization. For congregations, this means that a member of the governing board may also be the primary volunteer leader for the youth committee or the stewardship committee or any other committee formed to carry out the ministry functions.

Figure 1 represents the structure of a church whose governing body is a work group. The work group board traditionally consists of several elected board members who have specific responsibility for serving on or heading a committee. Figure 1 illustrates that these committees are offshoots of the board. The committee meets to address topics within its area of responsibility, and the committee representatives who are elected board members meet as a board to address topics of concern to the whole body. A typical church work group board could have committees on evangelism,

youth, education, and so forth. The senior or solo pastor position and staff positions are noted with question marks because, as we will see later, their official relationship to this type of board is unclear.

Often called a committee structure, this system of governance has been used by various denominations for specific reasons, but the system has some serious drawbacks as well. These reasons for and against utilizing a committee structure are described below. As you read, identify events or incidents from your recent experience with your governing body that support or contradict the comments below. The comments presented are drawn from discussions with many pastors and lay leaders in North America and western Europe.

**F**or most small congregations, this is a way not only to make management decisions but also to get the work done. The group decides on a plan of action and assigns the appropriate committee chairperson to carry it out. That person has a supporting committee to assist in accomplishing the work, and so the task is completed. Comments:

_____

_____

_____

_____

Figure 1

BUILDING

STEWARDSHIP

EDUCATION

FINANCE

FUTURE PLANNING

WORK GROUP
(Church Council, Board, or Governing Body)

EVANGELISM

PERSONNEL

MUSIC

YOUTH

FINANCIAL SECRETARY

SENIOR/SOLO PASTOR

?

STAFF

_____

_____

_____

_____

Frequently, however, the committee seeks or is given the power to make decisions that the board as a whole then simply endorses. Many times the other board members feel that the "experts" serve on the committee, and since they have studied a question, they must know the answers. The board is poorly informed, and committees seek power.

Comments:

_____

_____

_____

_____

_____

The congregation is able to utilize the many gifts and talents within the congregation for its own benefit. A banker in the congregation may be elected treasurer. A CPA may be elected to the auditing committee. A school teacher may be the director of education. A parent of teens may be the youth director. A soloist may be the chairperson of the worship and music committee.

Comments:

_____

_____

_____

_____

_____

_____

Frequently, however, the expert has a personal feeling that directs the focus of the committee and that may differ from the needs of the congregation. The soloist might like a particular style of music and use his or her position to promote this style alone. The banker may direct all ministry activities by simply saying, "We don't have any money." Private agendas, or the practice of seeking to direct activities based on one's own goals and wishes, are very common on a work group board.

Comments:

_____

_____

_____

_____

_____

The work group structure tends to abuse power in the congregation. Persons seek positions on the board in order to ensure that their own ideas are pushed through. (Incidentally, a board member legally holds the power of the position only when the board is called to order in official session. Outside the meeting, the position carries no authority to act or direct.) Some people seek the power that comes from these positions for their personal gain (recognition, getting their way). But Jesus said we are to seek service, not power.

"You know that the rulers of the Gentiles lord it over them. . . . It will not be so among you; but whoever wishes to be great among you must be your servant."
—*Matthew 20:25-26*

Comments:

_____

_____

_____

Frequently, a person may be well-suited to a particular position but cannot see the big picture in order to make well-founded governance decisions. The youth director may be able to manage a great youth program but unable to understand financial reports.
Comments:

_____

_____

_____

_____

_____

_____

Decisions at work group board meetings are frequently emotionally charged. Decisions that may be for the best of the congregation often affect the members making the decisions. How can the board discuss updating the youth program when the youth director, who has devoted so much time to the existing program, is present? How can anyone question

the treasurer's priorities when that person is a well-respected banker or financial planner?
Comments:

_____

_____

_____

_____

_____

_____

This style of governance involves members of the congregation. People like to be involved. With the many committees, there is a great opportunity to involve people in one way or another.
Comments:

_____

_____

_____

_____

_____

_____

At times, people have not been correctly chosen for a particular committee position. How can you "fire" someone who has been elected by the congregation, even if that person fails to carry out his or her responsibilities? Removing poor performers on the governing board is hard enough and may cause a great deal of pain in a congregation.

Comments:

_____

_____

_____

_____

_____

_____

Unfortunately, people are busy. While people are being encouraged in their busy lives to simplify by saying no to more and more demands on their time, congregations are finding it increasingly difficult to find faithful volunteers to keep a committee functioning. People view a lot of committee work as a waste of time. They don't have time for it anymore.
Comments:

_____

_____

_____

_____
_____

Involving the members in a democratic process allows consensus on deciding how ministry should be done. It builds ownership in the decision.

Comments:

_____
_____
_____
_____
_____
_____

Many times, ministry decisions should not be made in a democratic process. Mission and vision are two examples. Decisions need to be made by mature Christian leaders who are truly seeking God's will for the congregation. That may not be a majority of the congregation. God told the Israelites to take the land that had been promised them through Abraham long before. The democratic vote was ten to two against. The vote did not yield the right decision.

Comments:

_____
_____
_____
_____
_____
_____
_____

People need to be involved in the ministry, but it is far better to involve them in the _doing of ministry_ rather than in the decisions on _how to do ministry._ A committee may decide what programs the care ministry should offer, but people find greater fulfillment in giving care to those in need. A committee may decide to hold a youth retreat, but the sponsors and adult leaders will find greater joy in being with the youth on the retreat.

_____

Then Jesus summoned his twelve disciples and gave them authority over unclean spirits, to cast them out, and to cure every disease and every sickness. . . . These twelve Jesus sent out.
—_Matthew 10:1, 5_

_____

Comments:

_____

_____

_____

_____

Comments:

_____

_____

_____

_____

_____

_____

The committee structure maintains an orderly and logical way to sustain the ministry. It is stable and predictable. It has worked for decades. It allows proper deliberation and discussion over the questions that arise.

Comments:

_____

_____

_____

_____

In most cases, the current work group structure has evolved over the years to fit the needs of the congregation and maintain the status quo. Therein lies the problem. The organizational structure should be in place to meet the needs of people. As the true story of the new youth director whose welcoming party was delayed for months demonstrates, the requirements for committee review and deliberation at the expense of meeting the needs of people are wrong. Red tape is no excuse for poor ministry.

The structure is slow and cumbersome. It takes a long time to make decisions through each of the committee steps. It tends to prevent due deliberation and limits discussion. Committees cannot respond rapidly to the needs of people and end up preserving, protecting, and promoting the needs of the organization rather than meeting the needs of people.

Comments:

_____

_____

_____

_____

_____

Comments:

_____

_____

_____

_____

_____

_____

_____

The twelve came
to him and said,
"Send the crowd away. . . . "
But he said to them,
"You give them
something to eat."
They said, "We have no
more than five loaves and
two fish—unless we are
to go and buy food for all
these people."

—*Luke 9:12-13*

 **F**inally, and there is no "upside" to this point, the lines of responsibility to the senior or solo pastor and his or her staff are totally confusing in a work group style of governance. When the youth program grows to the point that it requires a staff person to coordinate the activities, to whom does that youth director report? The senior or solo pastor should be the senior staff person, and the youth director should be a professional. Does the youth director report to the pastor or to the chairperson on the youth committee? This is one of the biggest problems encountered with this type of work group board.

Quite frankly, what has happened over the years is that congregations have combined the governance with the management. We are trying to make decisions affecting the entire congregation from a mind-set of one particular volunteer position. We are trying to find people gifted in ministry management and make them governing board members. We are encouraging people to seek positions of power rather than positions of servanthood. This has caused and is causing great pain in congregations.

While some congregations have effectively struggled with these issues, and the structure is apparently working well for them, such congregations are a rarity and are rapidly becoming extinct.

Just as people in the business community have found that they need to respond quickly to the needs of their customers if they are to remain in business, the church needs to realize that it must respond quickly to the needs of its people if it is to retain them *for service* in the ministering community. In this post-Christendom paradigm, our members and visitors have the option to simply go down the street to another church or, worse still, to no church.

AN ALTERNATIVE TO THE WORK GROUP STRUCTURE

The answer is simple: divide the responsibilities of the governing body and the volunteer ministers.

More and more congregations are finding that they can establish a "board of ministries" to act as quasi-staff for the senior or solo pastor. Their responsibilities are to be the primary volunteers in their areas of ministry.

They may retain a working committee if necessary, but the committee only assists them in carrying out their volunteer role. Such a committee is not a decision-making body of the church. When the budget and needs of the congregation determine that a staff person should be hired, the volunteer holding the position may be asked to interview for the position. Slowly, as the congregation and ministry grow, the volunteer board of ministries becomes the staff, and board of ministry meetings become staff meetings. If a person is unable or ill-equipped to manage the

ministry, he or she can be quietly replaced or moved to another position without great public disturbance.

The role of the governing board becomes that of governance only. It is no longer involved in management. The role of management is assumed by the senior or solo pastor and the rest of the ministry team. (We'll talk more about management later.) The governing board in effect becomes a board of directors. This is illustrated by figure 2.

2. *Plan for the future.* The mission and vision of the congregation has been established. The governing board, as "trustees" of the vision, determines how the vision is to be accomplished. Strategic planning is the systematic approach of viewing the future and taking the steps on a year-by-year basis to reach that vision. Then, as the vision is nearing completion,

The four major responsibilities of the governing board are to set policy, to plan for the future, to monitor and evaluate ministry, and to lead the congregation.

strategic planning means setting in motion a review of the vision and establishing a new vision. The strategic planning effort will be covered in more detail in chapter 3.

1. *Set policy.* The governing board translates the responsibilities outlined in the governing documents into operating policy for the congregation. If the documents require the board to make sure insurance is in force, the board establishes a policy requiring the staff or the board of ministries to review insurance programs periodically. The governing board sets personnel policies concerning holidays, vacations, compensation, benefits, working hours, sick leave, and so forth. The governing board sets the policy and holds management responsible for its implementation. The governing board does not do the management.

3. *Monitor and evaluate ministry.* As elected leaders, the governing board members must be accessible to the congregation. The congregation should be able to air complaints and make suggestions. The board members should be looking at the ministry performance not as watchdogs but as persons truly interested in the quality of the ministry produced.

In addition, as the board plans for the future, the board holds the staff accountable for the accomplishment of the strategic plan action steps.

Figure 2

GOVERNING BOARD

SENIOR OR SOLO PASTOR

YOUTH

EDUCATION

BOARD OF MINISTRIES

PERSONNEL

MUSIC

EVANGELISM

STEWARDSHIP

STAFF

The board monitors itself to determine its overall quality and to take actions necessary to improve itself. It investigates governance structures and ideas that can improve the way the congregation carries out its mission and vision. *Total quality ministry* is one such idea, encompassing various management styles and techniques to bring overall quality ministry.

4. *Lead the congregation.* Your governing board members are the elected leaders of the congregation. As leaders, they are called to *lead.* It is true that the congregation will never grow beyond the leaders. They set the standards to which others will look. You can ask your congregation to tithe, but if the board members are not tithing, the congregation will follow their example rather than your exhortation.

A congregation might encourage its members to mature in faith and demonstrate it by

- **regular worship attendance,**
- **daily prayer and devotional life,**
- **growth through Christian education classes or seminars or involvement in small groups**
- **commitment to tithe,**
- **sharing their faith and being involved in missions.**

If this is what a congregation expects of its members these qualifications should become requirements for service on the church governing board.

Determine what kind of governing requirement you desire for your congregation:

_____

_____

_____

_____

_____

_____

_____

_____

Will your governing board members lead the way?

Take time now to review the membership on your governing board. If your structure currently combines both management and governance, make three lists. In the first, identify those on the board who are able to see the "big picture" of ministry, who are mature Christian leaders, who can see the mission and vision and enthusiastically support it, who place the needs of the congregation at a higher priority than their own desires and wishes. These are governing board members.

In the second list, place those current board members who have great gifts and talents in the area of ministry management. Here you will place your leader of worship and music (if he or she is particularly gifted in that area) or your youth committee chairperson or your evangelism chairperson. People are placed here as the beginnings for your board of ministries. Make sure you can work with these individuals as staff reporting to the senior or solo pastor.

In the third list, place those current board members who fit in neither category. Perhaps they should be removed from both management and governance and shown a place in which their individual gifts may be utilized. Sometimes these persons require additional training in order to be more effective. Sometimes they simply need to discover their spiritual gifts and be placed in an area in which they are gifted.

Place your current members into one of the three lists below.

You may need considerable help to bring about a change such as this. Only the governing board can change its structure. You cannot force it to change. The leadership on the current governing board must see and understand the benefits of such a change or be in such pain over the existing systems and processes that change will be welcomed. Many congregations today are in this pain but are not aware of remedies such as this. At times, you may need to bring in an outside expert or consultant or trainer to assist the board in seeing what is necessary.

GOVERNING BOARD	BOARD OF MINISTRIES	OTHER
1.	1.	1.
2.	2.	2.
3.	3.	3.
4.	4.	4.
5.	5.	5.
6.	6.	6.
7.	7.	7.
8.	8.	8.
9.	9.	9.
10.	10.	10.

Assuming now that you see and are willing to make the change in your style of governance, how does management take it from here?

MANAGEMENT

When the governing board is reorganized as a board of directors, it is in a position to empower others. When the purpose of the governing board is to set policy and hold management accountable, it must authorize and empower the senior pastor to make decisions and take risks.

The governing board is no longer involved with the day-to-day decisions, and this is liberating. One of the biggest difficulties in this transition for a board is recognizing that they can't know everything that is happening. A popular phrase from the marketplace today states, "Only hire people you trust; and when you do, trust them." Once you have hired trustworthy people, recognize that they are professionals, and treat them accordingly.

The senior or solo pastor is in most cases the senior staff member and fills a role similar to the chief executive officer in corporations. The governing board makes its policy and planning decisions and works with the senior or solo pastor and holds him

With the governing board reorganized in this manner, three changes will be evident:

1. The mission and vision will take a higher priority than private agendas.

2. The needs of people will take a higher priority than the needs of the organization.

3. Persons will want to be on the governing board to seek service rather than power.

or her accountable for carrying out these decisions. The board does not work with individual volunteers or staff members unless the senior pastor is involved.

In cases in which the senior or solo pastor is not particularly gifted in management or administration, the congregation may establish a management team.

In this case, the role of each member of the team is clearly identified and documented. Still, the board does not directly deal with any individual staff or volunteer person.

Are you as the senior pastor (or, if you are not the senior pastor, is the senior pastor of your congregation) equipped and gifted to manage a team of compensated staff or ministry volunteers? _____

If the answer is yes, then continue with the design of your management organization. If the answer is no, determine who may be assigned to assist in a management team and outline the duties and responsibilities of each of these people.

Your team of compensated staff and uncompensated volunteer ministry team leaders will be your primary resource for accomplishing ministry and mission. Its design is not simple or standard. Your starting point should be your mission and vision. Design your organizational structure in a way that maximizes your resources and energies in accomplishing what God wants you to do and become. The next few chapters will assist you in developing this design.

When we feel our congregational structure doesn't fit anymore, we should not look to find a structure that "feels good," nor should we look for a structure that is canonized throughout a region or denomination. We

Steve's son turned thirteen this year and has entered his growth spurt. It is very difficult to keep him in sneakers—his only choice for shoes. It is a lost cause to try to buy dress shoes for him, and besides, soon he will be able to wear his dad's. When shopping for his shoes, a comfortable fit is important, but it is also important to find a shoe that will allow him to be as active as he can be.

should be looking for a structure that equips us for action. A "feel-good" structure is usually one in which the needs of the organization are taking the highest priority. The accomplishment of our mission and vision should take highest priority, and that does not always happen in the structure with the greatest comfort.

CHAPTER

BUILDING A CHAMPION-SHIP TEAM

Thomas came to his new post at the church with great excitement. His interview process was very positive, and he was now the director of a major ministry area. There were a few concerns over his theological emphasis, which was slightly different from that of the pastoral staff, but his enthusiasm and tremendous gifts overshadowed these concerns. He assured the church leaders that he could easily minister under their direction. He soon convinced the leadership of the need for additional personnel in his department, and his ministry organization grew. His talent and personality granted him great favor among the ministry volunteers, and soon his popularity led him to boldness with his theological point. Ever so slightly, he was leading his ministry away from the mission and vision of this particular congregation. As he was confronted by the pastor on these issues, he became very defensive and rallied his supporters against the pastoral leadership. He demanded a hearing before the governing board, and as they listened to his accusations, the board members wondered how things could have gone so wrong.

His departure was very troubling for the congregation, but the overwhelming support of the church's mission and vision carried it through. A valuable lesson was learned: *You cannot have a championship team unless you hire champions who are in complete alignment with the mission, vision, and values of the congregation.*

WHAT ARE THE STEPS IN BUILDING A CHAMPIONSHIP TEAM?

I. KNOW YOUR NEEDS

For a small church of one hundred in worship, usually only one pastor is needed as full-time staff member. By the time the ministry grows to three hundred in worship, the staff is often augmented by positions such as a part-time youth director, a part-time adult education director, a part-time custodian, a part-time assimilation director, a part-time nursery director, and a part-time secretary.

Church leaders frequently ask, "Who should be hired first?"

It depends on your needs.
How do you decide your needs?

It depends on your *mission and vision* as described in your *strategic plan.*

A. Strategic Planning

Strategic planning is the process of building a structured plan that focuses the ministry toward the accomplishment of the vision. We saw in chapter 1 how important vision is to the congregation. We discussed in chapter 2 that long-range planning is a task for the governing board. A crucial part of that strategic plan will involve the hiring or appointment of team-mates.

If you attempt to separate vision casting and strategic planning from the decision to add volunteer or paid staff, you will likely slip into the bureaucratic mode of filling slots on committees with more warm bodies. In other words, without casting a new vision and planning strategically for a different way of doing ministry, you might not change anything but terminology.

In essence, a strategic plan will take a long view (typically, five or more years) into the future. The *vision* will set the tone in that it answers the question,

What has God called us to become?

After the team organized by the senior pastor has developed a vision statement, the governing board and staff (compensated and key volunteer positions) work with this statement to turn it into specific steps for the congregation.

"Have you not heard that I determined it long ago? I planned from days of old what now I bring to pass."

—*Isaiah 37:26a*

The vision statement presents a complete view of the future. As you begin the planning, the vision is the starting point. Each person involved in the strategic planning effort is in tune with the vision. The whole planning effort frequently returns to a discussion on the vision. This will keep the focus of the entire group.

As each person relates the vision to his or her particular area of service, individuals begin to interpret the vision personally.

What needs to happen in music and worship for the vision to be accomplished?

What needs to happen in missions for the vision to be accomplished?

What needs to happen in adult education for the vision to be accomplished?

"For which of you, intending to build a tower, does not first sit down and estimate the cost, to see whether he has enough to complete it?"

—*Luke 14:28*

As the answers are formulated in a general, long-term perspective, they become ministry *objectives.* Each objective is tested to ensure it is in alignment with the mission and vision.

VISION ⟶ OBJECTIVES

Note that lack of resources—finances, personnel, physical space, or anything else—is not identified yet as a limitation. Rather, the objectives are established, and these resources are then planned to support the objective.

For example, one congregation decided through strategic planning that it would relocate four years later. When a suitable piece of property was identified, the team went to negotiate with the owner of the land. During the negotiations, he asked, "How much money do you have to put down."

"Nothing," the team had to reply. It was true. The church had nothing.

That soon changed, because *what God decides, God provides.* If finances had dictated this congregation's future, the prime property would not have been purchased, and construction would not be in progress.

If you determine first your vision, *stick with this decision.* Then determine how it will be accomplished. Resources such as finances, staffing, physical space, and so forth will be listed as objectives necessary to achieve the vision. Then, *never* let the problem-solving stage interfere with the decision-making phase. Always make the decision, then solve the problems that the decision creates. As one wise person said, "If I waited until all the lights turned green before I went on a trip, I'd never go anywhere."

Your vision leads the ministry; finances don't.

From your vision, identify at least one major objective you know must be achieved in the next three to five years.

_____

_____

_____

_____

_____

Now you are ready to plan the steps necessary to achieve each of these particular objectives. You will establish goals based on these objectives. While objectives may be more abstract in terms of aims, feelings, attitudes, and atmosphere, the goals begin to interpret specific steps and time lines.

_____

_____

_____

_____

_____

> ## Not that I have already obtained this or have already reached the goal; but I press on to make it my own, because Christ Jesus has made me his own.
>
> *—Philippians 3:12*

The goals then are translated into specific annual action plans. An action plan determines what has to happen in the next year to make reaching the goal a reality. For each goal, there may be several action plans.

GOALS ⟶ ACTION PLANS

OBJECTIVES ⟹ GOALS

or the objective you identified above, list some goals you know must be achieved in the next one, two, or three years.

or one of the goals you identified above, prepare an outline of an action plan to be accomplished in the next year.

_____

_____

20346

_____
_____
_____
_____

When the action plans are achieved, the goal is achieved. When all the goals are achieved, the objective is achieved. When all the objectives are achieved, the vision is reality!
In one congregation, the steps work out as follows:

Vision

"To create the most imaginative Twenty-First Century Mission Center—bringing joy to the world."

Objectives

There are several supporting objectives to the vision. One is, "*Mission and Outreach:* To reach out in an innovative and loving way to the people living within thirty minutes of our church with the Good News of Jesus Christ. Keep missions at the heart of the church. Our target will continue to be the unchurched person. The new site will enhance this objective."

Goals

There are several supporting goals for this objective. One is, "Establish a missionary training program for youth and adults in three to five years."

Action Plans

Again, there will be several action plans to be accomplished within the next year to support reaching this goal. One is, "Within the next year the youth involvement in missions will be strengthened through establishment of a regular bimonthly mission opportunity trip to an orphanage in Mexico."

At the conclusion of the strategic planning effort, you will have a document that helps to direct all important decisions of the congregation. If you are to accomplish the vision, the energy and focus of the congregation needs to remain on the strategic plan.

If you intend to build a set of championship ministry teams, begin discussions now with your leadership team to complete the work on your strategic plan. Begin to schedule time for a retreat to discuss in detail.

My date for the discussion with the leadership team: _____

One objective in the strategic plan will now be the resources: specifically, the employed staff and volunteers necessary to accomplish the ministry objectives. *This is the starting point for your championship team.*

Through strategic planning, a staff position on this team has been planned long in advance. The position needs to be filled in order to accomplish the vision for the congregation.

Although strategic planning is necessary for the accomplishment of the vision, it is mal-

POSITION	TEAM RANK	YEAR
1.		
2.		
3.		
4.		
5.		
6.		
7.		
8.		
9.		
10.		
11.		
12.		

You may have more positions in mind; if necessary, use another sheet of paper to list them all.

to blur your vision. When the best-laid plans are thwarted, strategic planning is not the only source for determining your staffing and ministry team needs.

Whether or not you have completed a formal strategic plan, you probably do know the help you need to carry out your ministry and mission and when that help will be required. (Yes, having it yesterday would have been helpful.)

Consider the next three to five years. What team members will you need to add? On the table provided, enter these voluntary and compensated positions in the left-hand column. When you have listed them all, reread your mission statement, and rank the needed teammates in the order that you sense is most important. In thinking about the fulfillment of the mission, don't forget to add supporting staff such as secretaries or data entry persons.

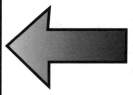

Next to the team rank, add the year that you need or desire this person to start.

B. Identifying Needs

You may be presented with opportunities to add staff persons through means other than strategic planning. After a Sunday morning message, a parishioner tells you how your message struck a responsive chord and met a need in her life. You note that others have also mentioned this to you. These discussions of a particular need might suggest a program

leable. New ideas and methods are developed and carried out. Some of the activities you try may not work as planned. Some action plans may not be completed due to circumstances beyond your control. The strategic plan should be reviewed at least annually so that you can name those chaotic things that seem for which you need help. This may lead you to think of a particular person who might be able to fulfill that role as a staff member or a volunteer.

God's call for meeting a special ministry need may lead to an individual presenting himself or herself to you as a particular gift important to your congregational body. The individual may be seeking a means to exercise this gift for the greater good of the body.

New members suggest that they have observed a particular ministry in another congregation which has worked wonderfully. They might volunteer to begin such a ministry in your congregation.

There are unlimited possibilities of how opportunities may be presented to you. There is a word of caution, however. If the need for a person or ministry is not identified in all the planning, prayer, and preparation you have completed in strategic planning, it may be a distraction rather than a gift.

My people have been lost sheep; their shepherds have led them astray, turning them away on the mountains; from mountain to hill they have gone, they have forgotten their fold.
—Jeremiah 50:6

We do not limit the work of the Holy Spirit in raising up persons to meet the needs of the body. However, whenever someone else suggests a ministry or person to begin the ministry always ask several questions:

Will this person or position help us accomplish our mission?

Will this person or position help us realize our vision?

Will this person or position help us fulfill a need that is important to our ministry?

If the answer to any one of these three questions is no, creating the position is a distraction of the ministry from its mission and vision. Your energy and resources could best be utilized elsewhere.

The hand of God was also on Judah to give them one heart to do what the king and the officials commanded by the word of the LORD.
—2 Chronicles 30:12

Return to your list above. Are there additional positions or persons that need to be added?

II. DECIDE WHETHER YOU NEED PAID OR UNPAID SUPPORT

In your work above, you listed the numerous positions you need to support your ministry. Should these positions be volunteer support or paid staff?

Ministry teams require management to provide direction, planning, scheduling, resources, training, and recruiting. You might be providing all this management yourself at this time and wondering how you can juggle it all, or you might have some volunteer or paid management help (for example, a youth ministry team leader).

Ministries also require teammates to carry out the goals of your mission by using the resources and training provided, in ministering firsthand (for example, the ushers or greeters).

As you consider hiring staff or finding volunteer help, you should first determine the function and purpose of the proposed staff person or volunteer. A staff person is not simply a paid volunteer! Some medium-sized congregations are experimenting with paying gifted "volunteers" a part-time wage. For example, the "volunteer" youth team leader in a church of four hundred in worship might be paid $10 per hour for ten hours of team management work each week. This approach is wise for a year or two, but if the "volunteer" is an effective team leader, the pressure

mounts from the paid "volunteer" or the governing body to make the team leader into a full-time staff person. This is a good problem to have if the worship attendance is increasing so that there is enough financial support to expand the staff. It is also a good problem to have if your youth ministry is a primary means of fulfilling your mission. If you do continue the practice of rewarding volunteers with a part-time wage, take care to remember that the role of a staff person is quite different from that of a volunteer. And this role can be complicated in the small- to medium-sized church if the paid person is both staff member and volunteer.

Simply put, *a staff person manages the ministry teams; a volunteer does the ministry.* As you move from hybrid roles to hiring full-time staff, it will be crucial to teach new team leaders (and the governing board) that the positions to be filled by paid staff members should be those that will help strategically manage the ministry—not those who will do the ministry.

As an example, consider the Christian education of children. The role of the children's ministry director would be to develop the children's education program, including the development of resource material, the recruiting and training of teachers, classroom preparation, and budget management. Whether paid or accomplished through volunteer support, this is a management position. The question is, At what point should this volunteer management position be changed to a paid staff position? What sort of confusion among the ministry team leaders ensues if some volunteer managers are paid, and others are not? It depends on your mission and objectives.

The role of the children's ministry teachers, on the other hand, is a volunteer role. A congregation need not turn these positions into paid staff positions. A few of the well-established (and wealthy) Sunday morning churches in larger cities have paid children's staff, but this practice (usually pursued at churches near universities, which emphasize adult ministries rather than youth or children's ministries) is likely to fade as congregations rediscover their mission and restructure their activities into self-directed ministry teams.

While reviewing the options in organizational management in chapter 2, we suggested that the ministry management team could be organized as a board of ministries. The team members could be either paid or unpaid. In either case, their function remains the same: they are support personnel for the senior or solo pastor to carry on the ministry of the congregation. These positions may change from unpaid to paid positions when any of the following things happen:

A. The work involved becomes more than a volunteer has time to do.

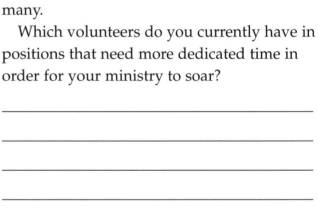

In most cases it will be time to hire staff when the work increases over twenty hours per week. Some dedicated volunteers will work beyond this, but not many.

Which volunteers do you currently have in positions that need more dedicated time in order for your ministry to soar?

_____

_____

_____

_____

_____

B. The accountability for work completion becomes intentionally evaluated.

Although volunteers are essential for ministry, volunteers are more likely to make their volunteer area a more flexible priority than other job- or family-related activities in their lives. Consequently, their urgency to complete tasks and manage ministry may not

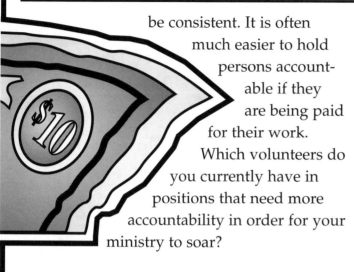

be consistent. It is often much easier to hold persons accountable if they are being paid for their work.

Which volunteers do you currently have in positions that need more accountability in order for your ministry to soar?

_____

_____

_____

_____

_____

_____

C. The task requires special skills and abilities that may not be available through volunteers.

Many volunteers are extremely gifted and dedicated individuals. However, there may not be many available in your congregation who have an education in elementary childhood education to be a children's ministry director. Also, there may not be anyone available who has the education and experience in finance it takes to be the financial director.

That is why it is important to take an honest inventory of every person and find out which volunteers you currently have in posi-

tions that need additional special skills or abilities in order for your ministry to soar.

_____

_____

_____

_____

_____

_____

D. Lines of authority and responsibility need to be focused and sharpened.

In many congregations, particular volunteers have been managing ministry areas for so long that people believe they are the primary decision makers. This is particularly difficult for a pastor responding to a new call. However, in any effective congregation, the senior or solo pastor ought to have the authority to lead and direct all paid and unpaid personnel.

Which volunteers do you currently have who challenge your leadership or authority and need to be released in order for you to enable your ministry to soar? (You may wish to omit writing names here or use "code" names.)

_____

_____

_____

_____

_____

_____

_____

_____

_____

_____

When the decision is made to make the transition from volunteer management support to paid management support, you will have the opportunity to broaden the selection options for the position. While there still may be a limited number of skilled volunteers available, there may be a much larger pool from which to choose if the position is to be a paid one.

As you plan the ministry development, the transition from volunteer management support to paid support should also be planned. It will be necessary to plan the financial resources you will need in order to make this transition a reality.

Now that we have explored some of the ambiguous issues about hiring paid and volunteer staff, you may wish to return to your list of the positions you wish to add and consider changes.

III. HIRE CHAMPIONS AS EMPLOYEES

You have determined to hire a person to fill a particular position. What steps should be next?

A. Create a written *job description.*

Writing the description requires that you consider carefully what you need. Think about the special *qualifications* you seek in the individual: education, skills, personality, experience, interpersonal skills, writing ability, compatibility, attitudes, faith maturity level, and so on.

Think about exactly what this person will do, for whom it will be done, who will provide supervision, what the salary range will be, what (if any) benefits will be provided, and what will be the working hours. Identifying these points in writing allows all potential candidates the same understanding of what will be required.

The following pages provide a sample outline for a job description. Tailor it to fit your congregation.

JOB DESCRIPTION
FOR THE POSITION OF
_____

FOR [YOUR CHURCH'S NAME]
_____

[Scriptural basis for this position]
_____

Prepared by: _____

Date: _____

In general, the job description is created *before* the person is selected for the position. Therefore, the description does not include a person by name.

B. Conduct a *search* for possible candidates.

The volunteer who has been filling the unpaid position may or may not be a candidate. Because this is a professional position, you might be able to generate a significant list of candidates, many of whom may have had considerable experience in a similar position.

JOB TITLE

FUNCTION: A brief description of the actions for which a staff person is being employed and of the role the person will occupy within the church's organization.

QUALIFICATIONS: A statement that describes the qualities or abilities required of a person in this specific position or task. The statement will include any educational qualifications and any required experience relevant to the position. Specify which qualifications are requirements and which are desired qualities. Specify whether the individual must be a member of the congregation.

SUPERVISION: The person to whom a person in this position reports. This will include administrative supervision and should also indicate others from whom job activities might be directed.

DUTIES AND RESPONSIBILITIES: A specific list of activities, services, functions, tasks, expectations, products, and anything else required by this position. Attempt to include all areas in general terms.

ADMINISTRATIVE: Identification of expected number of hours per week to be worked, the salary range (not a specific amount), whether benefits will be provided, and other such items.

You may seek the advice of other pastors you know. Perhaps they have gone through the same process you are now entering.

C. Conduct formal *interviews* with the potential candidates.

Each candidate should be interviewed by several persons either individually or as a group. Each person will have a different viewpoint and may perceive characteristics others miss. If possible, allow some of the primary volunteers in the ministry to participate in the interview.

During the formal interviews it is important to discuss the candidate's theological viewpoint and his or her reaction to your mission statement. Be aware that a candidate who strongly desires the position offered might tailor his or her responses in a way that suggests stronger support than they actually feel. Attempt to determine a true feeling and understanding through additional or more probing questions.

At the time of the interview, you might consider administering certain tests to the candidates. Personality and psychological testing may be helpful in determining whether the person will fit the position or will work with the congregation. It will also give you an idea of what style of management this person prefers.

D. Conduct *reference checks.*

You should always talk with the previous employers of the person you are considering hiring. They may be quite helpful in confirming impressions you form during the interviews, or they might identify a personality totally unlike what you identified. Reference checks help you identify whether candidates are indeed who they say they are.

E. Take this *responsibility* seriously.

Finding the resources and finding the right person to fill a position are exciting times, and you will be anxious to complete the search and hiring, but you do have key responsibilities in this process.

1. You have a responsibility to hire the best person available for the position.

It may take you time, but your congregation needs the best person available. The best candidate is not always the person who has been filling the position as a volunteer. It may be diffi-

cult for you to hire another when this person also desires the position, but find the best candidate and justify your selection.

2. You have a responsibility to safeguard your congregation from persons convicted of crimes.

Churches are a target for those who molest children. Churches offer molesters an opportunity to be close to children in an atmosphere of expected trust. Churches offer thieves and others who prey on people the same environment. Make it part of your employment process to be aware of these problems. Screen dangerous candidates by asking questions about their court and criminal records, and conduct the necessary background and reference checks.

NOTE

You should have a personnel policy manual that provides the specific terms of employment. That is, salary ranges by position should be specified, along with information about vacation time, holidays, personal time off, medical and dental benefits, life insurance, and pension. In addition, the policies should address reimbursement for household moves and interview trips.

3. **You have a responsibility for stewardship of the congregation's resources.**

As a steward of the congregation's donations, you will be expected to invest these donations wisely. The best candidate for a position is not always the first candidate interviewed. On the other hand, you may not have unlimited funds to pay for interview trips.

4. **You have a responsibility not to discriminate against individuals on the basis of sex, race, or any other factor that would not hamper job performance, and a responsibility to ascertain whether the person can legally work in the United States.**

If you have any questions at all, you may wish to discuss them with an attorney who can provide you with more specific information and individual state requirements regarding equal opportunity employment and employment of legal immigrants.

Now that you have hired a new management team member, celebrate! Find ways to publicly welcome and recognize the new person: a reception, an open house, an announcement during worship. Provide an orientation guide to help him or her get started. Provide support, direction, and assistance. Quickly determine the amount of coaching and direction this new team member needs from you in order to explore and use the gifts given him or her.

IV. PLACE VOLUNTEERS STRATEGICALLY

Volunteers are an essential part of your ministry teams. The selection and placement of volunteer support is critical, for it will determine whether or not a team can become self-directed in its opportunities to minister.

Frequently, congregations search for volunteers simply to fill needed positions as ushers, Sunday school teachers, youth leaders, caregivers, and all the other many ministries of the congregation. While the nominating search is noble and well-intended, the results of the nominating process are often dissatisfying for both the volunteer and the ministry teams.

Recently, Walt was speaking in a church in the Midwest. As he entered the worship center and proceeded up the aisle to the front, he was blocked by the head usher. "Where are you going?" he asked. Walt explained his purpose and was reluctantly allowed to pass.

A short time later, Mary Kallestad entered the worship center and also proceeded toward the front. Also blocked and questioned by the head usher, she was allowed to pass after explaining her need. She heard the head usher mutter softly, "If everyone gets to sit where they want, what's the purpose of my job?"

A. Create job descriptions for volunteer positions

What's the purpose of my job?
That is the first question many volunteers will ask. When seeking volunteers for min-

istry teams, anticipate their questions; ask yourself, What is the job? What skills, qualifications, gifts, abilities, or experiences will be necessary to fulfill this need?

Matching people with gifts to positions needing those gifts will result in meaningful and successful volunteer team ministries.

Writing job descriptions for paid staff requires us to really think about the position to be filled. The same care and thought should be used in preparing for volunteers. A volunteer job description will be very helpful, but it works best if the volunteer team member is coached in writing his or her own description.

Even if you follow the recent advice of church consultants to do away with written job descriptions, the question "What's my job?" still needs to be answered. For ushers, the position certainly requires the Sunday bulletins to be distributed. People need to be seated. The offering needs to be taken. Communion needs to proceed smoothly.

These are duties required of the usher, but they do not define the job of the usher team.

The ushers' primary purpose is to provide *hospitality*. Ushers and greeters are your public relations persons. They serve primarily to welcome and greet people—to make them feel special and cared for. They are to assist in making the worship service a great experience for the member, guest, and friend. Their job description should emphasize qualifications and gifts in hospitality.

When searching for teachers for adult education classes, interpersonal skills may be more important than knowledge, being humble may be more important than being correct, hospitality may be more important than control, imagination may be more important than information.

First, identify the foundational purpose and function of each position. This will help determine the best volunteers to fill these positions, and it will be a guideline for coaching teammates in owning their own tasks and activities.

Take some time to think about the following positions. What are the true purposes and functions of these positions? What gifts should be sought?

POSITION	PURPOSE	GIFTS
1. Nursery worker		
2. Offering counting team		
3. Sunday school teacher		
4. Phone caller		
5. Adult education teacher		
6. Youth group bus driver		
7. Volunteer coordinator		

Add your own list of volunteer positions and determine the purpose and gifts needed.

1.		
2.		
3.		
4.		

B. Match volunteers to team ministries

Our first step is to consider the needs of the volunteers. While the ministry certainly needs the volunteers, the congregational member or associate needs to volunteer. People find fulfillment in volunteering when they are exercising their God-given abilities for the building up of the body. When people genuinely feel they are making an important difference, it becomes a pleasure to serve. In the movie *Chariots of Fire*, 1924 Olympic gold medalist Eric Liddell says, "God made me fast. And when I run it gives God pleasure." Liddell got pleasure from giving God pleasure. Volunteers who find it a pleasure to serve have been matched perfectly.

In our society, time is often more valuable to people than money. People are being encouraged to say no to things that take their time. They are being encouraged to determine a personal mission and develop a personal mission statement. When asked or invited to participate in something that is not aligned with their personal mission, they should say no. Often this no comes in response to requests for volunteering.

However, when the volunteer opportunity is in alignment with an individual's personal mission, the ministry supports the personal mission and the volunteer finds the greatest satisfaction. The best way to align a volunteer opportunity with an individual's personal mission (which you may not know) is to determine the gifts and abilities of the congregational member and place that member where the gifts may best be utilized.

Instead of placing the volunteers where the ministry needs them, direct them to places where they are gifted to serve. They are much more likely to be successful and fulfilled in this volunteer role.

To determine the best place for a volunteer to serve, we start as we did in determining our personal mission and the mission of the congregation. We assist the potential volunteer teammate in determining his or her **SHAPE.**

is for **spiritual gifts**. Provide an opportunity for your members and guests to determine their spiritual gifts. This is the starting point. They may discover gifts of which they were not aware or may discover that those areas of service that have been the most rewarding in their experience are also where they are best gifted.

is for **heart**. Where is the heart of the volunteer? Is the volunteer's heart for disadvantaged persons, for children, for youth at risk, for seniors?

is for **abilities**. What special abilities does the person possess? Is he or she gifted in the use of hand or power tools, the computer, speaking, teaching, and so forth?

P is for **passion**. What provides the driving motivation in the person's life? What would he or she rather be doing than anything else? This is another way of asking, What is the call to ministry in the volunteer's life?

E is for **experiences.** What life experiences mold the character of the volunteer? What painful experiences have provided learning opportunities that can be shared with others?

Placing volunteers effectively will require the time to determine the volunteers' **SHAPE**. A volunteer coordinator should be gifted in human resource management to most effectively assist volunteers in determining their **SHAPE**. Once this is done, the administration of placing volunteers where their **SHAPE** matches the ministry need may proceed.

This process is not finished the first time a volunteer is placed in a ministry team. Continually carry on the process of determining volunteers' **SHAPE** in order to rethink your process for placement of volunteers. Outline the new processes that you will take to discover the gifts of your people and match

them to volunteer opportunities. Avoid using the same system for gift discovery for more than three to five years. There are many useful resources for discovering gifts that will renew people's desire to be in vital team ministry. Go back to the list of volunteers and gifts you just identified. Think about who is currently in each position. Does that person possess the gifts you identified? Plan to determine each person's **SHAPE.**

Building a championship team requires a great amount of hard work and preparation. Team ministry is not just a buzzword. It takes thought and study. It takes time and resources. It requires that the ministry first determine its mission and vision in order to find those who are most appropriately gifted and excited to be on the team. It is much more difficult and costly to remove and replace team members who do not fit or who contradict the vision than to take the time to adequately prepare for the new member. Invest in your volunteers and paid staff before they arrive, and it will be a more effective and enjoyable experience for everyone.

CHAPTER 4

CREATING A QUALITY ENVIRONMENT FOR YOUR TEAM

The senior pastor of a large congregation was very interested in establishing a high quality ministry for this congregation. He believed that the ministry management team of the congregation would greatly benefit from studying the principles of *total quality ministry*. These principles are derived from the literature of the quality movement, inspired by W. Edwards Deming, that has reformed the global business community. For total quality ministry to move beyond studying to implementing a different way of acting in ministry, the pastor knows that empowerment of every team member, staff and volunteer is essential.

Team members function at their best when they are empowered by ministry management to utilize their talents and abilities.

The key is for the paid church leader to coach rather than direct. The team members need authorization to question the status quo. They have a right to expect legitimate answers. Each individual is expected to make suggestions for improvement. Each is allowed to take risks without fear. The ministry teams are self-directed—by the mission of the congregation.

As the pastor talked about the benefits of this way of behaving in ministry with the staff, on his desk was a coffee mug imprinted with the words, "I'm the boss, that's why!" This mixed signal was very confusing to the staff. Another mixed signal was sent by the designated parking spaces that are next to the front door, covered by a roof, and marked by painted signs proclaiming, "Reserved for Senior Pastor," "Reserved for Youth Director," "Reserved for Worship Pastor."

There are several keys to creating a quality environment for your team. The first is to create an environment of *trust*.

TRUST

Trust is "assured reliance on the character, ability, strength, or truth of someone or something" (*Merriam Webster's Collegiate Dictionary*,

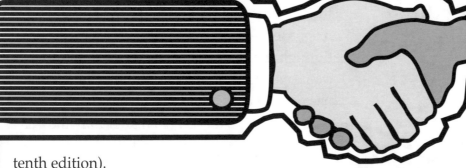

tenth edition).

Trust is an emotion frequently defined by its absence rather than its presence. Trust is gained or earned through personal contact, trial, testing, or interaction. People trust one another because of collective experiences with one another. The "assured reliance" comes through repeated contact and confirmation. Ministry team members trust or don't trust their leaders on the basis of repeated experiences.

As people work together, they develop a sense of one another's character, abilities, or strengths. They evaluate their level of trust based on what they observe. If you observe a person make errors in spelling, you won't trust that person to help you spell, although you might fully trust that person in other areas. If a person you know is always late to events, you will not trust him or her to be on time for anything.

Once trust is developed, it hurts terribly when the trust is broken.

Because congregations are supposed to be communities of love and joy, people often expect congregations to have no problems with trust. But it is often in congregations that people are afraid of hurting or offending others, and thus they do not speak the loving truth. As

we will see in this chapter, failure to be truthful destroys trust.

FACTORS INVOLVED IN TRUST

C H A R A C T E R

Contrary to what some politicians may say publicly about competence and charisma, character does matter. What a person does in secret or away from work is important. It all supports or detracts from trust.

> High standards for effective leaders cannot be compromised. Every church, every political structure, every enterprise private or public will never be any more disciplined than its leadership. Therefore, for a leader, moral and ethical discipline is not optional—it is essential. An effective leader knows that his or her private life is a public matter. What leaders do in private shapes their habits. If their private lives are morally healthy, they will lead with morally healthy habits. If, privately, a leader compromises the highest Christian values, morals, and ethics, then that leader will self-destruct.[1]

1. Walt Kallestad, *The Everyday, Anytime Guide to Christian Leadership* (Minneapolis: Augsburg Fortress Press, 1994), 42.

Character is the sum total of the internal values and beliefs that direct our behavior. We act in response to these directions.

For it is shameful even to mention what such people do secretly; but everything exposed by the light becomes visible.

—*Ephesians 5:12-13*

Some essential character traits that ought to be nonnegotiable are integrity, loyalty, honesty, discipline, and humility.

☑ *Integrity* is essential for trust. Today, many leaders, especially those who must be reelected each year, believe that the situation should determine the ethical response. However, integrity is discerned through the story that a person's life tells by example. The ethical values in this living witness do not depend on situations or circumstances. No matter how the person's lived story may be told, these values are visible at all times.

How do you define trust, in terms of trusting others to do their part in ministry? Name some "character words" that are important to you (for example, integrity).

1. _____
2. _____
3. _____
4. _____
5. _____
6. _____
7. _____
8. _____

Integrity is reflected when actions match words. When a promise is made, is it kept? When a statement is made, is it the whole truth? Does a person act differently when he or she is away from home—where no one is checking out the story?

When one's actions and words do not match, integrity is questioned, and mistrust develops. Questions are then raised concerning other things the person has said or done. Think about situations you've encountered in which integrity was questioned and mistrust has developed.

☑ *Loyalty* is another essential character trait. So many relationships are broken when one feels betrayed by another. When loyalty is suddenly questioned in a personal relationship, anger and hurt are the frequent responses. Likewise in a religious organization, lack of loyalty to one another or for the organization will lead to distrust and ill-feelings among the members. It is not surprising that church members' loss of loyalty to their denominational agencies and programs is the result of many decades of mistrust between the leaders and the members. The more the trust grows dim, the more the leaders behave according to their own agendas, for their self-interest grows strong and stubborn. Integrity is very difficult to restore in these social connections.

☑ *Honesty* is an important character trait. Honesty includes both telling the truth and being fair. People expect fair treatment. Prejudicial behavior either in favor of or against a person is not fair and will be detected by others. People will wonder if they need to gain your favor in order to receive fair treatment. The aspect of truthfulness is discussed in more detail below.

☑ *Discipline* is one's internal drive to train one's mental, moral, and physical abilities by instruction, control, and exercise. The training is revealed when testing comes. One is disciplined when situations or circumstances do not sway one from making the prudent moral decision.

> **Athletes exercise self-control in all things; they do it to receive a perishable wreath, but we an imperishable one. So I do not run aimlessly, nor do I box as though beating the air; but I punish my body and enslave it, so that after proclaiming to others I myself should not be disqualified.**
>
> *—1 Corinthians 9:25-27*

☑ *Humility* is the desire to emphasize one's activity but not oneself. The recognition of the team is more important than that of the individual. A humble person is not weak or insignificant but rather is driven from inner strength and conviction. He or she does not need the acclaim of others to be fulfilled.

> **Before destruction one's heart is haughty, but humility goes before honor.**
>
> *—Proverbs 18:12*

A B I L I T Y

Along with character, a quality team also needs ability.

Every congregation has at least one individual who believes he or she has a soloist's voice but in reality does not. That person is not trusted to sing, because he lacks the ability. It doesn't mean that he is a bad person, but he should probably be encouraged to use other abilities.

In like manner, people who are placed in positions of responsibility but who lack the ability to carry out those areas of responsibility will not be trusted. There will be no "assured reliance" on such people when their lack of ability becomes apparent.

Thus, no matter how much risk is placed in self-directed teams, it is imperative that when persons are interviewed for staff or volunteer positions that care is taken to clearly identify the job requirements and qualifications and ensure the candidate meets those conditions.

Jesus said, "For it is as if a man, going on a journey, summoned his slaves and entrusted his property to them; to one he gave five talents, to another two, to another one, to each according to his ability."

—*Matthew 25:14-15*

Continued training (see chapter 5) is also important in order to ensure the people keep their skills and abilities sharp. Advances in technology soon cause many important skills to become unimportant. What happens to the typist who cannot understand computers? Communication breaks down. What happens to teachers who are unable to operate a VCR? The curriculum is perhaps not as interesting or relevant to persons who no longer learn from lecturers.

As you think about your key volunteers and staff, consider the abilities they possess. What abilities need to be sharpened? Which of your volunteers and staff need to be encouraged to change positions because they do not have the abilities needed in their current positions? Make your notes here or on another sheet of paper, but do it now, while you are thinking about it.

_____

_____

_____

_____

S T R E N G T H

There is a game that is often played on retreats, in which one person is challenged to allow himself or herself to fall backwards into the arms and hands of another. Without seeing the other, the person who is falling must be able to trust the other person to have not only the willingness but also the strength to catch him or her.

In questions of trust in a team environment, strength doesn't always refer to physical might but also to stamina. The determination to carry on, to complete tasks, to not only start well but also finish well, to persevere in the face of difficulties are signs of stamina.

So let us not grow weary in doing what is right, for we will reap at harvest time, if we do not give up.

—*Galatians 6:9*

In the 1992 presidential election, Ross Perot lost a great deal of trust when he withdrew from the race. He was perceived as a quitter. Although he later returned to the race, he had lost a considerable amount of support. If he quit once, could he be trusted not to quit again?

Consider people in your congregation who have quit before completing a task. Have you trusted them with other important tasks?

When thinking about who fits where, it is sometimes easy to assume that a person with disabilities would not have the stamina or strength to function on a particular ministry team. But you might find that a disabled person has more perseverance than any other. Think about persons in your congregation who live in pain or discomfort. On what ministry team

could they be challenged to persevere?

Again, trust is the "assured reliance on the character, ability, strength, or *truth* of someone or something."

T R U T H

The character trait of honesty is essential for trust. Honesty can be very difficult for people. People tend to see truth in varying degrees. Consider some of the ways we try to rationalize and justify dishonesty:

Outright lies are thought to be wrong, but are "white lies" wrong? (After all, white lies are told to protect people from hurt.)
Partial answers that withhold information aren't lies, are they? (After all, the part of the answer that was given was true.)
Exaggerations merely embellish the truth a little and aren't really lies, are they? (People do need to see my point of view.)

They did not ask an accounting from those into whose hand they delivered the money to pay out to the workers, for they dealt honestly.

—*2 Kings 12:15*

Frequently, congregational members fear telling the truth because they don't want to hurt someone's feelings. The fact is that, often, withholding the whole truth ends up hurting more deeply.

Pastor Bob is talking with Ruth, a member of the congregation, about a lack of participation in the youth program. Pastor Bob attributes the poor showing to the youth director's lack of contact with the youth in the community. Suddenly the youth director rounds the corner and comes face-to-face with the two. Pastor Bob says how pleased he is with the work of the youth director.

While this may avoid hurt feelings and conflict for the present, the perpetuation of this lie will eventually cause greater hurt and conflict. It will lead to confusion when the truth is finally revealed and the director is surprised after receiving all the positive affirmation. It will lead to feelings of betrayal and bitterness.

This is hurtful not only for the youth director but also for Ruth. Would Pastor Bob also talk this way about her? Her feelings of mistrust may lead her to discuss this with others. Soon staff and volunteers cannot believe what Pastor Bob says, and his positive affirmation creates nothing but suspicion.

Lies destroy trust. Without trust it is not possible to have a healthy relationship.

Partial truths, withholding necessary information, and deliberate distortions or exaggerations are forms of lies.

"Hear, for I will speak noble things, and from my lips will come what is right; for my mouth will utter truth; wickedness is an abomination to my lips."

—Proverbs 8:6, 7

Another form of lying is to avoid conflict by speaking one way to one person and another way to a second person. The avoidance of conflict in this manner not only doesn't solve the problem, but also causes the problem to grow. The conflict is not resolved, and it will return. But this time it will be compounded by the lies.

If we are careful to know the truth and express it with grace and consideration, we are speaking with integrity. If we honestly approach someone with an issue or complaint with the desire to maintain relationships, the issue can be resolved without hurt feelings. **Quality fixes the problem—not the blame.** When deficiencies occur, the leader who is highly trusted focuses on the deficiency—not on the person. The deficiency can be corrected without personalizing the problem. Consider your approach to deficiencies and problems. Are you honest and forthright? Do you speak the truth in love? If two people with whom you have discussed the same issue get together, will they agree on what you said?

Consider your key staff and volunteer team leaders. Are they honest and forthright as well? Do they gossip about others? Will they tell you and one another the truth? Nothing will destroy trust faster than dishonesty.

R E S P E C T

Other factors affect trust as well. Each person is unique. God has created each person with gifts, abilities, and talents. Personalities develop. People are not alike. On almost any topic, intelligent and informed people can disagree.

Yet we are to recognize that all are created in the image of God. Everyone has special value in the Body of Christ. We are to respect one another even if we differ. Studying personality types on a retreat helps church staff members to understand one another and how we differ. It allows us to appreciate the gifts and the mix of personalities brought together by God. It allows us to develop a greater respect for one another even though our viewpoints may differ.

This leads to a greater feeling of respect.

MOTIVATION

Why do people do the things they do? Why do people desire to be staff members? If the motivation of someone is in question, everything else is in question as well.

In team activities, it is not always necessary that the motivation for accomplishing the task be the same for all participants. It is, however, important that each understand what motivates the others.

Some may be motivated by the sense of completed ministry. Others may be motivated by the income of the job. Others may be motivated by the completion of the task. Some may be motivated by personal recognition.

When a team member's motivation is hidden or suspected to be contrary to the overall motivation of the ministry, confusion develops. Even when it is contrary to the motivation of others, a motivation that is self-disclosed or revealed is much healthier and more acceptable.

ATTITUDE

Attitudes help to shape the way we view life and situations. Attitude is the window through which one views the world, the task, oneself and others. Attitudes can lead to trust or to mistrust.

As you consider the attitudes listed below, think about how the ones in the left-hand column lead to a more trusting relationship.

Sensitive	**Harsh**
Cooperative	**Solitary**
Fair	**Partial**
Open-minded	**Judgmental**
Respectful	**Prejudiced**
Hospitable	**Imposing**
Accessible	**Aloof**
Faithful	**Unfaithful**
Punctual	**Tardy**
Patient	**Impatient**
Encouraging	**Discouraging**

Consider then the attitudes in the right-hand column. Would you tend to trust or distrust persons with these attitudes? At the risk of opening old wounds, think of a person whom you do not trust. What attitudes above would explain these feelings? Have you prayed for that person?

Just as individuals are truthful, provide respect, express motivation, display character traits, and express attitudes, so do organizations. Congregations gain reputations in these areas as well. Congregational leadership displays these traits and can establish an environment where trust is fostered or one where it is not.

Trust is critical to the success of teams—whether governing boards, management teams, self-directed teams, or cross-functional ministry teams. Unfortunately, it is often the case that congregations suffer from a lack of trust just as much as for-profit corporations do.

BUILDING TRUST

Building trust is a matter of aligning these factors—character, ability, strength, truth, respect, motivation, and attitude—for each member of the team, whether paid staff or volunteer.

Trust on a ministry team can be established when

- each member agrees to tell the truth and believes others will as well;
- each member shows self-respect and respect for the other team members;
- each member identifies his or her motives for participation;
- each member displays his or her own character, and it is understood and accepted; and
- each member's attitude is exposed as positive and supportive of the efforts of the team.

Recall that the dictionary defined trust as "assured reliance." Assured reliance can occur only through repeated and frequent *personal*

contact with other team members. It is important to build up the emotional "trust bank" with the other team members so that when the occasional misstep occurs, each member has enough on deposit with the others so that trust is not destroyed.

The following "Team Contract" may be helpful for you and your key teams. Consider how you may use or revise it to suit your situation.

> **Trust in the LORD with all your heart, and do not rely on your own insight. In all your ways acknowledge him, and he will make straight your paths.**
> —*Proverbs 3:5-6*

EMPOWERMENT

Empowerment is the sharing of power—the sharing of the authority and responsibility to take action. Empowerment occurs when those who possess the power share it with clear guidance and focus.

Empowerment and trust go together. There is an old saying: "Only hire people you trust. Once you've hired them, trust them."

TEAM CONTRACT

As we work together on this team, we need to develop a deep sense of trust in one another. Trust is based on being truthful, being respectful, understanding one another's motives, possessing good character, and maintaining a great attitude.

As a starting point for this team, this contract establishes the ground rules and expected behavior for trust. Each team member will read and agree to the statements. If anyone disagrees with any of the statements, openly discuss this with the team.

1. I choose to trust each member of this team.

2. I am personally committed to improvement in our congregational ministry.

3. I am personally committed to improvement in my areas of responsibility and influence in this congregation.

4. I place a higher priority on the concerns and well-being of the congregation than on my own individual concerns and well-being.

5. I have a responsibility to God to fulfill my responsibilities in this congregation in the best way I can in accordance with the call that the Lord has placed in my life.

6. I will speak honestly and openly with each member of this team. I will speak the truth as I understand it. I will accept what others say to be the truth as they understand it.

7. I will respect the rights, gifts, talents, personalities, abilities, and other unique traits God has given each of us on this team.

8. I will listen to the input of others and give it fair hearing.

9. I will keep sensitive or confidential information private. I will not gossip about team members but will support and stand up for them.

10. I will contribute my best to the efforts of this team. I will carry out the assignments and support the conclusions made by the team.

Together **E**veryone **A**ccomplishes **M**ore!

Integrity requires us to take personal responsibility for knowing our own truth and expressing it in love and grace.

_____

(Name)

_____

(Date)

To update this wisdom, If you trust them, empower them. Place only volunteers you trust in positions of authority. Then trust and empower them.

500 Lb.

500 Lb.

500 Lb.

What is the best example of "power" in your experience with your congregation?

_____

_____

_____

_____

_____

_____

Who has power? Identify the person(s) by name or position.

_____

_____

_____

_____

_____

_____

_____

The pastor certainly has power as the religious leader. The presiding officer of the congregation has power. Each team leader has power. There are also members of the congregation who are not in elected positions but have

power. Power can be used positively or negatively, but power need not be thought of in negative terms. Power is a facet of every organization. Power is necessary in order to accomplish work. We need people to have the power and authority to take action in the best interest of the congregation.

Power is not bad. The abuse of power is. When an individual seeks power in order to force his or her own ideas and interests upon the congregation, the best interests of the congregation are diminished.

Many congregations have terrible internal battles that remind us of bloody power struggles. Persons have sought election to the governing board in order to gain power, to get their own way. A person may seek the position of worship team leader to determine who will sing during worship or which style of music will be presented. A person may seek to be treasurer to decide how the money will be spent.

[Jesus] said to them, "The kings of the Gentiles lord it over them; and those in authority over them are called benefactors. But not so with you; rather the greatest among you must become like the youngest, and the leader like one who serves."

—Luke 22:25-26

The Bible clearly instructs us to seek positions of service rather than positions of power.

Empowerment is the giving away of your personal power and the sharing of authority. The trusting, empowering leader assumes that power is not limited. To grant power to another does not diminish the power but multiplies it. It increases the effectiveness of the congregation, makes it tremendously more responsive to the needs of the people, and it builds self-esteem and self-worth among the team members. *See Figure 3.*

A traditional view of leadership in an organization emphasizes providing direction for the organization and its staff. That view would be high in the upper left on the diagonal of this figure, indicating high direction and low empowerment. An empowering leadership emphasizes involvement of the employees and workers. Consequently it is high on empower-

ment and low in direction (lower right on the diagonal). In actuality, situations can determine where on the diagonal line leadership operates, but the goal is to be near the lower right.

Empowerment changes the focus from manipulating team members to coaching associates. It encourages the teammates to use their own creativity and gifts to solve problems, to be innovative, to take risks, to succeed or to fail, and to learn from the success or failure. It sets parameters and goals and allows the associate the freedom to achieve those goals.

THE EMPOWERED CONGREGATION

In an empowered congregation, the church membership empowers the elected leaders to

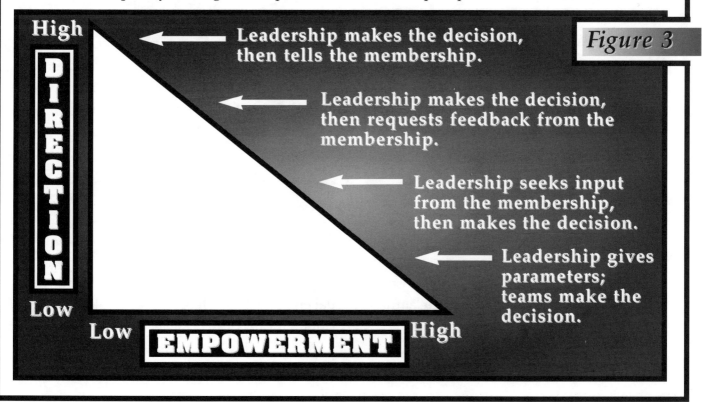

Figure 3

High

DIRECTION

Low

Leadership makes the decision, then tells the membership.

Leadership makes the decision, then requests feedback from the membership.

Leadership seeks input from the membership, then makes the decision.

Leadership gives parameters; teams make the decision.

Low **EMPOWERMENT** High

carry out their responsibilities. The church member continues in involvement, but is in support of the focus, the mission, and the vision of the congregation. The church member may express his or her personal agendas and ideas, but these always take a position in submission to the needs of the congregation.

Forums for discussion and meaningful debate are available. Also, there are opportunities for people to share ideas, frustrations, and comments. Methods are created for people to make their feelings known to the elected leaders. After participating in these forums and hearing from the congregation, the leaders are allowed to take action.

EMPOWERED LEADERSHIP

In empowered leadership, the elected leadership shares its responsibility with the management of the congregation. Power is not held by committee but rather is entrusted to the senior or solo pastor, the paid team leaders, and the volunteer leaders so that they can effectively accomplish the work of the ministry.

In an empowered congregation, the governing board does not give up its responsibilities but rather it trusts the pastor and his or her staff to carry out many of those responsibilities and holds the pastor accountable for those responsibilities. The staff then has the authorized freedom to take action and to risk. It has the right to make mistakes and to learn from those mistakes.

EMPOWERED MANAGEMENT

In an empowered congregation, the ministry management team enthusiastically shares responsibility with the individual employee and volunteer leaders to accomplish the mission. The management team members become mentors and coaches rather than directors. The management's role is not to control but to take away barriers for the employees and volunteers in order to allow them to carry out their responsibilities.

EMPOWERED STAFF AND VOLUNTEERS

In an empowered congregation, the individual employee or volunteer leader takes responsibility for his or her own actions. Personal quality is highly important. He or she makes decisions, takes risks, seeks advice, learns new skills, sets goals, monitors progress, makes improvements, contributes to team effort, and communicates as necessary.

Because the staff's role is management and the volunteers' role is ministry, an empowered staff and volunteer organization returns the power to the individual congregational member. The winsome cycle is complete.

The congregation empowers the board.

The board empowers the senior pastor.

The pastor empowers the staff and volunteers.

The staff and volunteers empower the congregation.

Whereas many congregations fight over which camp has the power, an empowered congregation spreads the power around and empowers itself. It unlocks the tremendous talent, gifts, abilities and passions placed within the congregation for its greater good.

SHARED VISION

Without positive direction, the congregation is unable to go anywhere. Without a unifying goal, there is chaos. Without shared vision, congregational power will be vested in personal feelings and personal agendas. Meetings will last for hours, and fights over limited resources will consume the people. Debate will take on a destructive, emotional nature.

The importance of the vision and the mission in creating unity was discussed in chapter 1. Acceptance of these basic factors

helps also to focus the power. With shared vision, those who may have personal agendas lose their abusive power. Sharing a vision makes it possible to do what God wants done. *Wanting what God wants is wanting what's most important!*

If you believe that God has a plan and a purpose for your congregation, then you must listen to God and seek what God wants. This focus guides the decisions and prioritizes the resources. This shared vision knows the source of its authority and provides the motivation so essential for meaningful mission and ministry.

These three tasks are essential for creating a quality environment for your ministry teams: create trust, empower people, and establish a shared vision. People will thoroughly enjoy serving and working in this environment, and your ministry teams will soar on eagle's wings!

CHAPTER

MAINTAINING A CHAMPIONSHIP TEAM

The courtship before marriage for most people is a very romantic and intimate time. Couples spend hours together talking about their dreams and feelings. They exchange special gifts. Each person devotes a great amount of time concentrating on the other and on their relationship. After the marriage this concentration may fade. This will cause the relationship to deteriorate. The key to a successful relationship is making the relationship a high priority.

The same concentration and commitment is essential in your relationship with your staff and volunteers. You have spent a great deal of time developing the relationship. You cannot start ignoring the relationship once it has been established. Relationships require constant maintenance.

Up to this point we have provided the foundation for developing quality teams in the congregation. You have discovered several things:

 A mission and a vision that are well-communicated shape the focus for the whole congregation and lead to unity among the ministry teams.

 The organizational structure that is set in place provides the management help and encouragement for the teams of staff and volunteers.

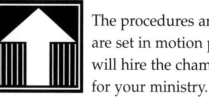 The procedures and policies that are set in motion predict that you will hire the champions needed for your ministry.

You have worked hard to create an environment of trust, empowerment, and shared vision. You have created a workplace where the gifts and abilities of your staff and volunteers can be unleashed. Your process for hiring or appointing has focused on character, competence, and commitment; it has helped people with passion discover their spiritual gifts and put them to use.

Now your task is to help your staff and volunteers discover and uncover these gifts and abilities. The secret to maintaining a championship team now is to provide opportunities for them to grow and develop. When the honeymoon between new staff and the congregation is over, what will keep the marriage alive and growing? Better yet, how can the honeymoon continue?

Members and associates will become frustrated and feel stuck if they cannot develop with the congregation. Competent people want to learn new things. They want to know what other successful ministries are doing. They seek the latest technological information to be most effective. Without personal and professional growth, they may look for opportunities elsewhere. Professional staff are always interested in their professional careers. The team of competent volunteers is eager to help but wants to grow at the same time.

How can you help provide the opportunities they need to grow and develop?

TEACH YOUR CULTURE

To illustrate, imagine that your ministry has been in desperate need of a youth director. The search has been a long process, involving much of your time and effort as well as

that of others to get the position filled. But at last, the chosen person is settling into the position, and you are now free to turn your attention to other pressing matters.

Wrong!

Your orientation time with this person is critical. The youth director needs time with you for positive coaching and direction. In an empowering organization, it is important for the staff or volunteers to understand relationships, authority, boundaries, expectations, and available resources. They need either your direct time or that of their supervisors to help establish these parameters.

Persons are often hired for their expertise. However, their expertise is not effectively unlocked until they understand the *culture* of the congregation. The culture is the unwritten, assumed set of rules concerning behavior and lifestyle within the congregation. How are things really accomplished? Who needs to approve actions before they can be implemented? How are financial resources unlocked? How does the phone system work? Where does one get office supplies? How do we communicate with one another?

A user-friendly staff and volunteer handbook may be a very useful tool for providing the essential information. Simply telling the answers or requiring the employee or volunteer to find out on his or her own is not sufficient. Spend some time on the enculturation phase so that the employee can get a

strong, successful start without unnecessary conflicts.

It is also important to consider how work is accomplished in your congregation. Put yourself in the position of a new staff person, or think about the last person you hired. Would you know how to gain approval for desired activities? Would you know how to gain approval to spend money? Would you know how much you could spend? Is there someone who makes the final decisions about almost everything?

Make notes of all the things that come to mind as you consider these permission-giving questions. Then ask the last person you hired if you could have provided information that would have better facilitated his or her transition into using the gifts he or she had brought to your congregation. Add these communication needs to your list. Make sure you have included these in your staff and volunteer handbook.

_____

_____

_____

_____

_____

_____

TREAT THE PAID PROFESSIONALS PROFESSIONALLY

Church staffs often grow as the needs of the congregation increase. Frequently, a volunteer is highly involved in a ministry area until the need arises to hire a person for the position. Once the person is compensated for the work, the person becomes a paid professional. It is important to empower these staff persons for ministry.

As we discussed in chapter 3, you have made specific choices in the decision to make a transition to a paid staff. Whether because the position required a greater time commitment, because specific skills were necessary, because authority questions existed, or for other reasons, you now have a paid professional in this position. It is obvious but crucial that you respect this person as one worthy of his or her hire.

Honor, respect, trust, and empower your colleagues in ministry. A church worker knows when the senior pastor is arrogant, dictatorial, or condescending about credentials or experience. Certainly we are not suggesting that unpaid volunteers should be treated with any less respect for their contributions and skills, but the "psychological contract" shifts when a person is given money in exchange for performance in ministry. If that gift of revenue is not offered with honor and respect, your staff will become apathetic almost immediately.

To be professional, you should provide your staff with a well-organized policy or personnel manual. Employees need to know they are being treated equally and fairly. What is the vacation policy? Who receives benefits? Is personal time or sick time paid? Are holidays paid for hourly and salaried persons? How is compensation established? What are guidelines for conduct? How are terminations handled? Is there a grievance policy? Who does performance reviews? These and others are questions asked by professionals who dedicate their lives to a task.

Frequently, congregations determine that limited financial resources prevent them from paying staff at levels at which other companies in the community may pay for similar work. Do not apologize for the salary offered or accepted. As persons called of God to ministry, ministers and church workers make the decision to accept or not accept the compensation that is offered along with the position. An apology may be received as a signal that someone else may have been offered the job if a higher salary was available. It also might create the impression that part of the responsibility should be considered or continued as a volunteer role. This can be very confusing to the paid church staff member and to others.

Review your personnel or policy manual. Are the questions about compensation and benefits addressed? Are your employees

being treated fairly, or are special benefits or conditions afforded some but not others? Consider asking or surveying your present staff regarding their feelings about these issues. You might consider obtaining legal advice or advice from experts in human relations in your state to develop or update your manual.

PROVIDE FOR CONTINUING EDUCATION

To paraphrase Zig Ziglar, there is one thing worse than training a church worker and losing him or her to another church. That terrible thing is to not train the church worker and then keep him or her!

The dissolution of church staff is prevented by promoting lifelong learning in your congregation. With the rapid pace of change in our culture, most of the skills a student learns in college will be obsolete within four years of that student's graduation. With so much new information available to us every day, and with the shifting structures and systems that operate in the church, the church staff person could also become obsolete. People with new ideas based on new information will seek to replace those who do not grow. And no one wants to be obsolete. For example, throughout the twentieth century there has been a major movement toward making the directors of Christian education programs more professional. Schools for Christian educators were established. Degrees were granted. Professionally trained Christian education directors at the end of this century are seeing their numbers diminish, and some Christian education academies have been disbanded. Many Christian education directors have avoided obsolescence by learning how to manage a menu of church programs or by specializing in family ministries.

Steve purchased his first computer in 1982. It was state-of-the-art with two floppy drives and a large, 20-megabyte hard drive. Today it is obsolete. Today's state-of-the-art programs cannot run on that machine. The entire machine cannot even be sold at a flea market.

Modern computers can be upgraded. A computer with a 386 processor may be upgraded to 486 or pentium. A 4-megabyte RAM may be upgraded to 8 or 16 or 32 or even 64 megabytes. The computer will remain useful much longer if it is designed for flexibility.

In the same way, people do not become obsolete if they continue their training and keep from becoming territorial about what they already know. To avoid this kind of parochial attitude about gifts and abilities, you should provide training and education so that church workers are always seeing new possibilities for the application of their gifts. This does not always mean spending large amounts of money, although it may be necessary at times to send a

small group away to a learning event.

Computer programs are continuously upgraded with new versions that have new capabilities. One person familiar with the new features

can train others in the office who also use the program. Designate someone the trainer for each program. There may be one trainer for the word processor program, another for the spreadsheet program, another for the congregation database manager. The trainer also benefits by keeping up on the changes in order to conduct the training.

If staff are unavailable to do the training, there may be congregational members who can help. So often people say, "I never knew it could do that!" New features frequently lead to time savings or to creative ways of being more productive.

Encourage your staff and key volunteers to develop relationships with their counterparts in other congregations. These relationships may result in ideas of "best practices"—success stories that may translate directly or indirectly to this congregation. Frequently, congregations find that while another congregation may provide a mentor for them, they provide a mentor for another.

Every congregation has access to churches that have developed into "teaching congregations." These congregations have as part of their mission the development of best practices and the desire to provide training to others. Your congregation may also wish to join an association such as the Willow Creek Association or Leith Anderson's Mentoring Congregations.

Many major ministry areas have specialized annual conferences or training sessions. Children's ministry directors meet in one place. Music directors meet in another. Church administrators in another. The information available and networking that goes on at these conferences is of great value. (See appendix B for a list of some of the institutes and seminars that are available.)

Single-day conferences in cities around the United States are very popular, and most provide good training. Conferences for everyone from receptionists to directors to governing board members are available.

You may find that formal education is also valuable to some on your staff. A better understanding of adult or child learning methods may be important for the education director. A class at a local college might be helpful.

What continuing education opportunities have you taken in the past two years?

_____

_____

_____

_____

_____

What continuing education opportunities have you made available for your staff and key volunteers in the past two years?

_____

_____

_____

_____

_____

_____

Happy are those who find wisdom, and those who get understanding.

—Proverbs 3:13

PROVIDE NEW TOOLS

It wouldn't make much sense to hire a person with a master's degree in finance and provide him or her a slide rule for calculations. You wouldn't send a groundskeeper to mow a one-acre lot with a push mower. Improvements in technology help us do our work more efficiently. It is often difficult to keep up with the latest features. Just as the 1982 computer has become obsolete, the difference between the 286, 386, 486, and pentium processors in computers is amazing. Once one has worked on a 486, a 286 or 386 seems incredibly slow.

New computer programs have provided new tools for developing new skills as well. Desktop publishing and thousands of clip-art designs provide the opportunity for creating attractive brochures at each workstation. This no longer remains the job of one layout artist. In the past, many computer programs required extensive training and practice. Today, the programs have been upgraded with user-friendly icons and pull-down menus so that one is able to begin to use the program instantly.

The wide availability of computers has allowed many secretaries to become administrative assistants. As many church workers are using their own computers for their word-processing needs, the need for typing letters and other word-processing work by secretaries is declining. When the computer stores files easily, the need for filing diminishes. Secretaries who are learning new skills through continuing education while the old skills are in less demand will find themselves remaining useful and productive.

Phone systems with automated attendants can assist the church worker in time management. Although person-to-person communication is always best, all of us miss phone calls from time to time. Rather than simply playing phone tag, anyone can leave a brief message on voice mail, and the work can be accomplished without an actual voice-to-voice or person-to-person exchange.

Paging systems, personal beepers, and cellular phones allow a person to have greater physical freedom while still remaining connected and able to be contacted.

Be alert for new tools to provide your trained championship team. Continue to invest in your team's productivity. Often these new tools are the first to be dropped when you are preparing the next year's budget and your projected income doesn't match your expenses. Remember, you have invested significantly in these church staff members. It remains essential to provide them the necessary tools. The prices of

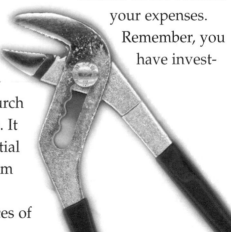

most technological tools have decreased so that they are affordable by most congregations.

Finally, consider the activities that consume large amounts of your or your staff's time. Are there new tools available that could reduce this time? If you had the new tool, would you be able to free up time so that a new project or task could also be accomplished?

_____

_____

_____

_____

_____

_____

SEEK THE INVOLVEMENT OF TEAM MEMBERS

People work best in environments that they help to create. It is easier to remain motivated and achieve goals when one has set these goals for oneself. It is easier to take action when one has contributed to the action plan. Some of the worst working environments in congregations develop when events, decisions, goals, or actions are thrust upon people without their input. When an individual participates in the decisions, planning, problem solving, goal setting, strategic planning, and other activities that directly affect him or her, the individual takes ownership of the needed actions.

_____

Then I got up during the night, I and a few men with me. . . . [A]nd I inspected the walls of Jerusalem. . . . Then I said to them, "You see the trouble we are in, how Jerusalem lies in ruins. . . . Come, let us rebuild the wall of Jerusalem. . . . " Then they said, "Let us start building!"

—Nehemiah 2:12-18

_____

Most congregations have found it helpful for staff members to be involved members in the congregation. Every staff member needs to be participating in the life of the congregation in the same way you expect others in the congregation to participate. The reality is that the congregation will never venture beyond the pace or attitudes of the leadership. As the leaders go and grow, so goes the rest of the congregation. Volunteerism for staff should be nonnegotiable.

One should not be excused from volunteer support simply because one works at the church. It is the staff member's church just as it is for others who participate. Staff involvement isn't volunteerism unless their efforts are in areas other than their expected contributions. For staff members, volunteer support means participating in activities other than those directly connected with their duties as staff members: the youth director teaching adult classes or the maintenance director singing in the choir or the data entry person serving as an usher. These are healthy and visible ways to reinforce the staff's high level of commitment.

Consider your current staff. Are they involved in the life of the congregation? Are they active in the decision-making processes that affect them? If not, consider how you can begin to increase their involvement.

BREAK DOWN BARRIERS

Deming has said that 85 percent of an organization's problems are caused by its management. That is, because management is responsible for the policies and procedures the employees must follow, and because most problems are a result of poor process or policy planning, management must be responsible. Your church

workers are responsible for only 15 percent of the problems. Once you admit that, you are on the way past fixing blame.

One major role for the church manager, then, is to break down the barriers that hold the church workers back from excelling.

> **For everything there is a season . . . a time to break down, and a time to build up.**
> —*Ecclesiastes 3:1, 3*

Fix the problem, not the blame!
Perhaps the music team does not work well

Paid Team Member	Volunteer Activities

with the youth team. This makes it difficult to plan youth choir trips. Management is responsible for removing the barriers that prevent smooth operation. Create an environment where the groups are expected to collaborate.

The adult education team leader at one church raised a concern in a staff meeting that there was too much red tape for paid church staff. When pressed for details, the team leader expressed a general frustration with paperwork. After the meeting, further discussion revealed that her specific frustration was with the procedure necessary for the design and mailing of advertising brochures and flyers. Through process mapping (the written identification of each step necessary to complete a process), the procedure necessary to mail a flyer was discussed and outlined. The team leader was correct. The process was cumbersome and there was a lot of paperwork! It was easy to understand how it had become that way. Each step in the process was placed there in response to previous problems. In solving the problems, however, the process became cumbersome and time consuming. Redesigning the process took time. However, it also presented an opportunity to consider problems encountered by others who were affected by the process.

The new process not only met the adult educators' desires to streamline the process, it also eased several other problems and yet maintained the integrity of the previous problem-solving

solutions. Barriers were broken down and the process was made more efficient.

Breaking down barriers is the church manager's responsibility. The goal is to assist staff and key volunteers to grow and develop so that more people may be brought together to love and serve God.

Never turn problems into excuses!

What complaints or suggestions have you received repeatedly from staff or volunteers? Investigate the underlying causes or effects of the problems, and you may discover a barrier that can be removed. Must team members go through a lot of red tape to gain approvals or to schedule events or to obtain custodial action? You might consider asking about this on a staff and volunteer survey.

RESOLVE CONFLICT QUICKLY

Congregational ministries involve people. Where people work together, there is bound to be conflict. Most conflicts can be resolved by the individuals involved. However, there are times when management must help. If the conflict is with the man-

agement, many unfulfilled expectations will emerge throughout the entire organization.

The first step in resolving conflicts is to acknowledge that the conflict exists and that something must be done. All too often, congregations either wait for the conflict to resolve itself or they deny that the conflicts even exist. If people are able to resolve their own conflicts in a mature Christian manner, management will not need to take action. However, this is too infrequently the case.

"So when you are offering your gift at the altar, if you remember that your brother or sister has something against you, leave your gift there before the altar and go; first be reconciled to your brother or sister, and then come and offer your gift."

—*Matthew 5:23-24*

Frequently, pastors are reluctant to take action because they fear they will be drawn into the conflict. The reality is that it is much better to face it than to hide from it. Ignoring the problem helps no one. Most often, ignorance allows the situation to deteriorate.

Always remember that the goal is to fix the problem and not the blame. The enemy is not the person with whom you have a conflict, but the problem itself. Try everything possible to avoid an adversarial role in resolving the conflict. It should not be you against the employee, but rather you and the employee against the problem.

With the working conditions and atmosphere you and your team have developed, you and your staff and volunteers are ready to soar! You

are now ready to work together cooperatively. You are ready to build teams. You are ready for collaboration!

CHAPTER

MINISTRY TEAMS IN YOUR CHURCH

Two are better than one, because they have a good reward for their toil. For if they fall, one will lift up the other; but woe to one who is alone and falls and does not have another to help. . . . A threefold cord is not quickly broken.

—Ecclesiastes 4:9-10, 12

Team is the buzzword for organizations at the end of this century. Executives extol the benefits of cross-functional work teams in designing new products or services. How does this relate to your congregation?

Teams in the corporate setting are very much like teams in the congregation. The collective abilities, talents, intelligence, and experiences of the team members make their collaborative efforts superior to those of any individual.

The organization of teams gets to the heart of organizational management. As we discussed in chapter 2, a management team may consist of staff or volunteers or both. It is the group of people who manage the ministry.

Through numerous discussions with congregations around the country, we have seen myriad ways of organizing ministry. In some congregations, the committees of the congregation hire the staff, who then take direction only from the committees. In others, only the pastor hires the staff, and all staff take direction only from him or her. In others, a more typical corporate model is used, in which the senior pastor takes on a role like that of a chief executive officer, with middle managers reporting to him or her and supporting staff reporting to the middle managers.

One common characteristic in all these congregations is that the staff

structure is like it is because "that's the way we've always done it." A better way to think about the organization of the management of the congregation is to ask the question, "What is the best way to organize this congregation in order to accomplish our mission and vision?"

If you had the opportunity to rethink and replan your congregation's management structure right now without thinking of the potential problems that might be encountered along the way, what would you do?

A PHILOSOPHY OF MINISTRY

The first step in developing a philosophy of ministry will be to determine who you are serving and what needs they have.

This may seem obvious or innate to your call as a minister, but let's consider the children. Certainly some of the children in your congregation are in the fourth grade. But all fourth graders are not the same. They are at differing levels of Christian understanding—some may have been in Sunday school for six or more years, and some may be new this year. Some fourth graders live in two-parent homes and others trade off each week between parents. Some may be brought to Sunday school every week and others once a month.

Consider the youth cultures: the needs and interests of youth vary greatly and change rapidly as adolescents mature. Consider college students: some are eighteen and some are much older, pursuing second careers. Consider singles: some are divorced, some are widowed, some live with their parents, some are professional students. Consider the diversity among adults.

You can extend from your mission statement (see chapter 1) to develop a philosophy of ministry by considering each of your constituent groups and determining how your mission is accomplished for each. That is, How is the mission of your congregation interpreted for the youth? How is it interpreted for children? How is it interpreted for singles?

Therefore, since it is by God's mercy that we are engaged in this ministry, we do not lose heart. We have renounced the shameful things that one hides; we refuse to practice cunning or to falsify God's word; but by the open statement of the truth we commend ourselves to the conscience of everyone in the sight of God.

—2 Corinthians 4:1-2

It might be helpful to consider each constituent group in a process. Identify the "raw material," the "finished product," and what needs to be accomplished in order to transform the "raw material" into the "finished product." Note, however, that the analogy of a manufacturing process is not entirely accurate when it is pushed into literal one-to-one comparisons. Church guests and members are not manufactured products on an assembly line. There are no "rejects" in this process. Each person is a special gift of God who is placed in our care. We Christians never quit when the task of transforming persons to love God is difficult or even apparently impossible.

For your youth, the "raw material" may be a seventh grade student totally new to the church with no biblical literacy. The "finished product" may be a senior who is mature in Christian faith, loves God and neighbor, and is able to nurture and be a mentor to others. Or the "finished product" may be one who is able to articulate a personal testimony of faith and who demonstrates the unconditional love of Jesus in daily life. The activities of the youth team will be determined as the *processes* that bring about this transformation.

As you plan your process for transforming the youth, it is also important to remember that you will be receiving a "finished product" from the children's programs. If the children's ministry has properly prepared the youth, it will be much easier and more rewarding to bring the youth ministry to the next level. Your definition of the process for each step in the life process needs to be carefully considered.

Take some time to consider the characteristics you see in your "raw material" and "finished product" for each of these constituent groups.

	"Raw Material"	"Finished Product"
1. Preschool (age 3-kindergarten)		
2. Elementary (grades K-6)		
3. Youth (grades 7-12)		
4. College age (18-22)		
5. Young adult (22-30)		
6. Young married (22-30)		
7. Young divorced (22-30)		
8. Young parents (22-30)		

Continue this exercise for each of your constituent groups. You may find overlap, but you may also find that there are unique aspects of either the "raw material" or the "finished product." (You will return to this chart later to determine what ministry programs will assist in transforming the "raw material" into the "finished product.")

Completing this activity will help you sharpen your focus on your philosophy of ministry. You will begin to see the integration of each of these areas into one whole picture. The preschool ministry blends into and builds on the elementary school ministry and that blends and builds into the youth ministry. The youth ministry blends and builds into the college age ministry and that blends and builds into the young adult ministry, and so on. You begin to see a lifelong development strategy emerging. This becomes your *philosophy of ministry*.

This also is the basis for your management organization.

JOB MARKET

singles. Congregations have these departments because they fit the philosophy of ministry when the ministry was organized in centralized denominational systems. Departmental thinking was the management philosophy of the corporate world too when denominations thought about a common structure or blueprint for congregations. The message is not that ministry departments are a bad system. However, we think that you will soon see that teams are better.

Happy are those who find wisdom, and those who get understanding, for her income is better than silver, and her revenue better than gold.

—*Proverbs 3:13-14*

MINISTRY TEAMS

Many congregations have developed departments for their major areas of ministry, such as children, youth, adult education, stewardship, evangelism, and

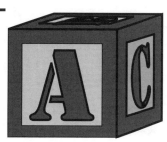

In any congregational structure, you need to depend on those who are experts in a particular ministry activity. No one church worker can be completely knowledgeable in all areas of the ministry. Thus one person will not likely have a great understanding of

the learning techniques both for eight-year-old students and for single adults.

This is why congregations departmentalize the management structure by placing staff or key volunteers as department heads reporting to the senior pastor or executive pastor. Each department head has a support base of staff or volunteers to assist him or her in accomplishing the department goals and ministry.

What follows then is the traditional hierarchical management structure seen in most corporations and reflected in most congregations. *See Figure 4.*

You may be able to place names of people in your congregation in the boxes below. In the previous section of this chapter, you identified the "raw material" and the "finished product" for each ministry area. Certainly one responsibility of the department head is to determine the programs necessary to transform the particular "raw material" into the "finished product." Department heads and experts are an integral part of this process.

The unfortunate result often is a departmentalized structure that builds *psychological* walls around the department and interferes with the cooperation between departments. There are congregations in your city or town in which one department head (lay or volunteer) will not speak with another unless directed or

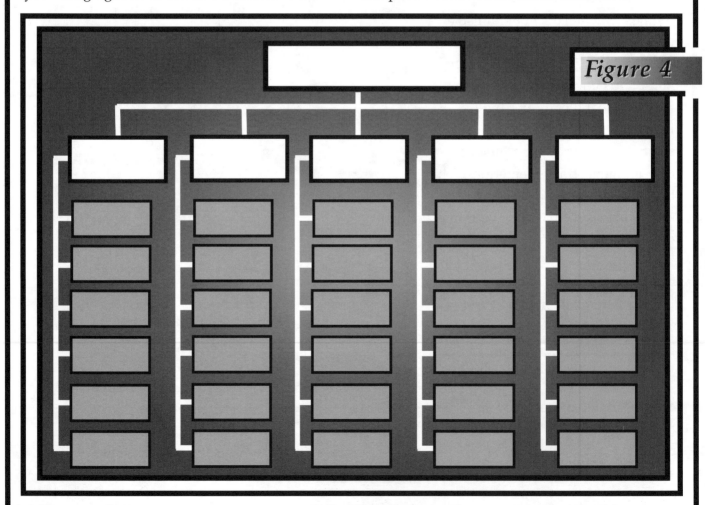

Figure 4

prompted by the senior pastor. Is your congregation like that?

Departmentalized organizations tend to physically locate each department's staff and volunteers together to facilitate their departmental work, which also then places *physical* walls around the department and further divides the management of the organization, even as it often encourages destructive competition between departments.

For he is our peace; in his flesh he has made both groups into one and has broken down the dividing wall, that is, the hostility between us. He has abolished the law with its commandments and ordinances.

—*Ephesians 2:14-15* a

Department personnel plan together, play together, pray together, promote together, and generally stick together. Members of one department may not even know members of other departments.

As members of a church staff or volunteer teams, if we do not get to know one another we miss seeing and utilizing the expertise, gifts, abilities, and perspective that each of us can bring. There is no collaboration. Also, people tend to mistrust people they do not know.

Ministry teams are formed by gathering the right people with the right expertise, gifts, and abilities to focus on a particular ministry area or problem.

At times the teams focus totally on the needs of their respective departments; for example, when the youth team is planning the ski retreat. This is our traditional view of departmental work. When the work is internal to the department, the team is called a *family* or, in some congregations, a *natural ministry team*.

At other times, it is desirable to gain expertise from several natural ministry teams. In the planning of a youth choir mission trip it would be helpful to have representation from the youth team, the music team, and the missions team. A group formed to plan this activity is called a *cross-functional ministry team.* Synergy between the various team members develops creative ideas for ministry that could probably not be identified by individuals working alone.

A management structure that encourages and enables this type of team approach to ministry will be the most effective.

Review the philosophy of ministry that you developed just a few pages ago. As you and

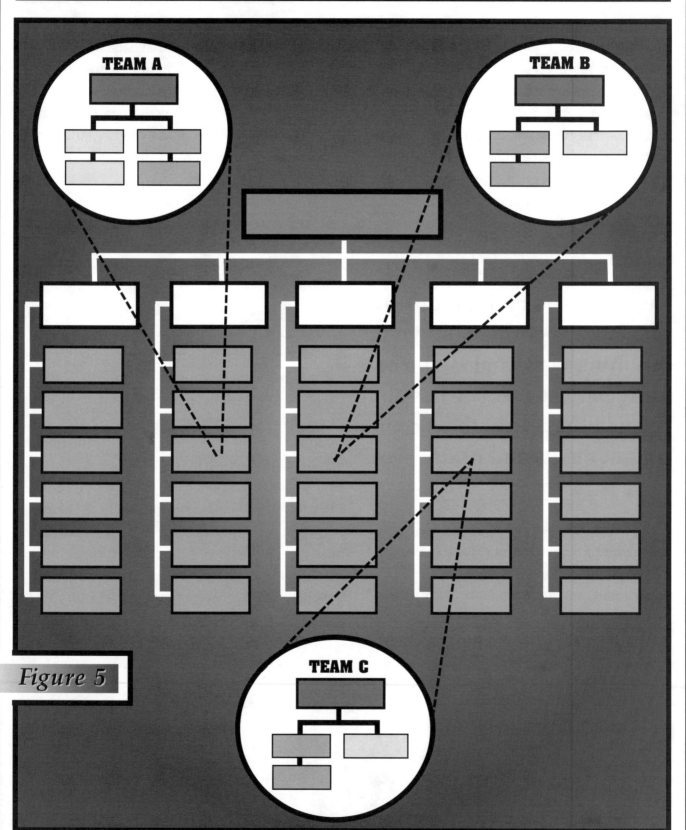

Figure 5

your natural ministry team leaders plan, you see again the integration of each of the areas into one whole picture. The preschool ministry blends into the elementary school ministry and that blends into the youth ministry. Planning overall strategy should therefore involve a cross-functional work team of preschool, children, and youth team members. How does each area contribute to the whole? Once the cross-functional work is completed, the family teams will develop the individual strategies for their work.

The youth ministry blends into the college age ministry, and that blends into the young singles, young divorced, and young parents ministry, and so on. The cross-functional team should have representatives from the youth, adult, singles, family ministry, small group, and other affected teams in attendance to develop an integrated strategy. Your life-development strategy is now taking shape through the teams.

Your leader of small groups may join with the youth team to plan small groups for youth. Your adult education director may join with the children's director to plan activities and classes for families with small children. Your seniors team leader may join with the singles team leader to plan activities for active seniors who are single. Your facilities manager may team with all these groups to assist in planning space for the activities.

These cross-functional ministry teams need not only include the department heads. Other staff or volunteers who are in supporting roles may also have special expertise to contribute. An administrative assistant for the youth team

may be especially gifted in organizing retreats. This person could easily join with the adult education team in planning an adult retreat. A data-entry person in the office support staff could join with the children's ministry to assist in setting up enrollment and attendance procedures.

A team approach to ministry breaks down barriers between departments and encourages cooperation. (Do you remember from the last chapter that breaking down barriers is part of your leadership responsibility?) When cooperation succeeds and is encouraged, collaboration occurs. This is the ideal state of work for staff and volunteers.

Cooperation allows a smooth operation between departments when each participant understands his or her role in the overall ministry and completes his or her responsibilities accordingly.

Collaboration occurs when each participant understands his or her role and completes his or her responsibility in such a manner that it enhances the work of the others.

Do nothing from selfish ambition or conceit, but in humility regard others as better than yourselves. Let each of you look not to your own interests, but to the interests of others.
—Philippians 2:3-4

TEAM FORMATION

It is your role or that of your department heads to form the teams when the benefits of a team approach to planning or problem solving is desired. There are several important ingredients in team formation.

The first of these ingredients is the precise identification of what the team is to accomplish. A specific program, event, expected outcome, goal, or problem statement is the starting point. The team will then clearly understand and focus on what they are to do. Unless the team meets normally as a "family," it is a waste of time to continue the team meetings after the goal has been achieved.

Once the goal or problem statement is clearly stated, you must identify the boundaries within which the team will operate. You may not want the team to address or change certain aspects of a situation, and this must be made clear before the team meets.

At the 8:15 Sunday morning worship service at one church, the attendees complained that the live band leading worship was too loud. The church leadership had already determined that the style of music at this particular service was not to be considered in resolving the issue, which meant that it was outside the boundaries for problem solving. The problem was solved inside the boundaries given.

Another ingredient is the identification of the relationship between the activities of the team and the mission and vision of the congregation. The team should understand how its work makes a positive impact on the church's overall ministry.

The time allowed to complete the project or solve the problem should be clarified. Deadlines and significant milestones are important as the team plans its work. Without a time constraint, many teams will continue to meet, without reaching their goal, until they disband in apathy. A pastor told us that his congregation had appointed a banner committee to make a banner for the church. After two years, the committee had still not decided on the style of banner. They wasted valuable human resources.

The team needs to understand its authority to make decisions and effect change. Is the team empowered to make change, or are they to make recommendations to the church's management? To whom shall the reports be made? Who has the final authority to act?

What other resources are available for the team? Are financial resources budgeted for the team or available if necessary? What personnel resources are permitted? Is a consultant needed? Are there other staff or volunteer persons with specific expertise? Do you have a staff person or a volunteer who is a skilled negotiator, arbitrator, or team facilitator who can roam among ministry teams as an expert in group dynamics? Are there books available? Is travel authorized? Perhaps some specific training would be helpful.

In summary, the essential ingredients for a successful team formation include

1. identifying the goals or expected outcomes of the team activity,

2. establishing the boundaries for the team,

3. identifying the relationship of team activity to the overall mission and vision of the congregation,

4. creating time constraints and deadlines,

5. clearly stating the authority of the team to make changes, and

6. providing the necessary resources for the team to accomplish its goal.

Consider a current problem area or a new service to be provided by your congregation. Begin to think of the people you could call together in a team to solve the problem or plan the service. Think about how you will provide the ingredients for team formation noted above.

TEAM PERSONNEL

The people you select for the cross-functional ministry team are very important. This selec-

tion process starts with the team leader.

The team leader should be a well-respected leader in the congregation and have the skills necessary to assist the team to reach a conclusion. The team leader will be coordinating and planning the meetings. He or she will lead the meeting, coordinate the activities, and provide direction to the team. If reports or records are required, they will be the responsibility of the team leader. The team leader will make sure assignments are understood and will follow up on their completion.

Your selection of team leader will depend on the situation. You may appoint the same team members from time to time and select different team leaders at different times.

The team leader's task is to encourage the team effort. Some may find it difficult to bite their tongues and allow the team to reach the best solution without imposing their own will on the team. If the team leader is also, for example, the youth director, he or she should leave his or her position as youth director outside the team meeting and participate as a team member.

Next, you will select the team members. Teams usually consist of less than eight members, but you will select the participants based on their individual expertise and the needs of the team. Be careful in your selection that you do not overlook someone who should be involved in the outcome. In chapter 5 we noted how important it is for employees and volunteers to be involved in the decisions that affect them.

It will be expected that the team members will participate in the team activities. The team leader should encourage participation by all members and limit the dominating members. Each team member should recognize that each person is personally responsible for the efforts of the team.

The following page suggests a form for team guidelines. Modify it as necessary to conform to your congregational use.

TEAMWORK

Effective teamwork occurs when all members not only carry out their roles but also enjoy their participation on the team because of the improvements and progress they are making. Team members learn to bring their own agenda items and become concerned not only with the results of the meeting and the task in which they are involved but also in the meeting process itself.

They enjoy the fellowship time as well as the business time. In addition to completing the tasks, they seek ways to improve the team meetings.

Achieving this level of participative teamwork requires several things:

- **Building trust.** Each team member must trust the others to accept him or her and his or her ideas. The team members also need to trust their management.

- **Enhancing communications.** Individuals need to be able to express themselves and be understood. Information should be readily shared among members.

- **Resolving conflicts.** When people are involved, conflicts may happen. They cannot be ignored.

- **Sharing a common vision and mission.** This is the unifying factor that makes sense of the activities of the team.

- **Building cooperation and collaboration** instead of competition among team members.

- **Unlocking the creativity within each team** member.

- **Rewarding the total team effort.**

- **Sharing responsibilities and empowering** members.

Effectiveness and quality in compensated and uncompensated staff requires **TEAMWORK!**

TEAM GUIDELINES

Statement of problem, goal, or expected outcome:

_____

_____

This statement relates to our mission, vision, or philosophy of ministry in the following way:

_____

_____

To achieve our stated goal, solve our problem, or reach our expected outcome, we will employ (✔ one)

❑ a cross-functional team   ❑ a natural ministry team

The following team members have expertise to serve:

Team Leader: _____

Team Members: _____ _____

_____ _____

_____ _____

_____ _____

_____ _____

_____

Team Facilitator: _____

The boundaries for this project:

Time constraints: _____

Process starting point: _____

Process ending point: _____

Financial resources: _____

Personnel resources: _____

Other resources: _____

Support and management assistance will be provided by and reports should be made to:

_____

This team does/does not have the authority to make changes within the boundaries noted above (circle one).

Additional information concerning this project is attached or can be found at:

_____

Training. Chapter 5 identified the importance of keeping up-to-date with skills and techniques.

 Empowering. An empowering atmosphere is important in order for team members to risk involvement in providing solutions.

 Assisting the process. It is the responsibility of management to help break down the barriers and obstacles that prevent smooth operation. Eliminate the compartments in the congregation!

 Motivation. Your mission and vision provide the starting point for motivation. The relationship between the activities of the team and the mission and vision are important for motivation.

 Winning attitude. In resolving conflicts between people or ideas, seek a win-win rather than a win-lose solution. A winning attitude unlocks creativity and imagination.

 Optimized resources. These resources include your people. Make sure your teams include the right people.

 Respect. Each team member must respect the others. Recognize that all are given different gifts and abilities. All serve the Body of Christ.

 Keeping in touch. Good, frequent communication is vital in establishing a teamwork approach to ministry. Team members must be able to communicate with one another, and the entire ministry staff and volunteer organization needs to be fully informed.

When the team has accomplished its goal, it can stop meeting, unless there is a good reason for the team to continue meeting on an ongoing basis. Wasting the time of busy people is one of the most deadly drains on commitment. Meeting for the sake of keeping the team meeting or for the sake of the leader's ego is an annoyance to everyone. Meet only when there is an expressed necessity to meet.

Where there is no guidance, a nation falls, but in an abundance of counselors there is safety.
—Proverbs 11:14

G od's desire is that congregations would use the gifts God has given them to the best of their abilities. People can use their gifts to the greatest benefit when they are placed effectively in teams in which they are involved, empowered, encouraged, and appreciated. The synergism and multiple talents in such teams result in better decisions, better programs, better plans, and better solutions.

CHAPTER

RECOGNIZING EXCEPTIONAL PERFORMANCE

One thing yet remains in building quality ministry teams: establishing a recognition and reward system that honors and encourages exceptional performance. *Exceptional* performance should be rewarded—not all performance. Intentional recognition of exceptional performance will raise the standard for all other performance. Those who perform exceptionally are usually driven by internal motivation and may not need the recognition (although they usually appreciate being noticed).

This kind of recognition occurs for the benefit of other staff members and volunteers. They benefit by seeing the high standard that is set and by observing that the one rewarded is deserving of the honor.

The key question is, How can exceptional performance be recognized, especially considering the limited financial resources of the congregation? It is first important to understand the demotivating concept of competition, and how competition can be eliminated in evaluating exceptional performance.

COMPETITION

Society values competition. Not all competition is good, however, especially when one staff member or volunteer is placed in adversarial competition with another.

Personnel evaluation systems that rank employees either formally or informally create competition—*competition for the highest position and the highest salary.*

Merit increases in compensation create competition, and merit increases based on personnel evaluations double the competition—*competition for the highest pay raise.*

Recognition systems can also create competition—*competition for attention.* Be careful that those whose positions are of a support or "behind-the-scenes" nature are not overlooked.

When the church leader attaches his or her

Take a few minutes right now to consider how you may be promoting competition in your staff or volunteers.

Do you devote more time to certain people than to others? _____ Name them:

_____

_____

_____

Do you tend to notice the more obvious performance and neglect those who are "behind the scenes"? _____

Does your compensation system favor certain church staff members over others? _____

Does the "squeaky wheel" always get the grease while the quiet ones go unnoticed? _____
What other areas come to mind where you or congregational systems may be unknowingly promoting unhealthy competition?

_____

_____

_____

_____

Be alert for signs of adversarial competition and discover how that competition is created. Then work to eliminate it wherever possible by appropriately recognizing and rewarding exceptional performance. Several systems are available for congregations.

career to the most visible and spectacular projects and neglects other, less visible projects, this creates competition—*competition for contact.*

Listening to the loudest or most frequently heard voices also creates competition—*competition for favor.*

Your employees and key volunteers are interested in a working environment where they are evaluated and compensated on the basis of their abilities and performance, not on the basis of the abilities and performance of others.

PERFORMANCE APPRAISALS

There are those who believe that all performance review systems run counter to the goals of empowerment and involvement. The introduction of personal bias and judgment into the systems will demotivate and disillusion employees. Regardless of the system used, competition for recognition, promotion, and rewards will result between individuals.

The negative aspects of performance evaluations must be balanced against the desire of conscientious, introspective, and dedicated church workers to receive honest feedback on their performance. While everyone likes positive feedback, most people, especially those interested in improving their own performance, want to know how their efforts are honestly perceived. In addition, it is the responsibility of congregational managers, as stewards of the church's mission, to monitor the work of employees and volunteers and provide feedback on their performance.

Therefore, it is necessary to provide some form of performance appraisal. What should this process include?

As you will see, the elements of a traditional performance appraisal process can be modified to create a more healthy, helpful process.

1. *Yearly feedback on employee performance.* Pitfalls in this system involve the bias of the evaluator and what is or is not visible to him or her. This system does not identify whether the employee has been properly trained, given the proper resources, or had tasks properly prioritized by the evaluator. Simple miscommunication and poor communication might have resulted in the employee missing the mark.

There needs to be frequent discussion between the supervisor and the church worker to verify or modify performance. Make sure the priorities and expectations of both the worker and the supervisor are clear. Assist the church worker in setting his or her own goals and objectives. Once the church worker has done this, empower him or her to strive to

meet those goals and plan for frequent conversation on his or her progress. While a formal evaluation once or twice a year may be necessary, the review should never be a surprise.

If a particular problem has been discussed, this needs to be documented immediately along with the corrective action developed by both the worker and the supervisor. Progress on that corrective action may then also be evaluated.

A performance appraisal should allow the worker to talk about his or her perspective of his or her own performance in relation to mutually developed and agreed-upon goals. Seek input from others with whom this staff member or volunteer works. If he or she is part of a team, gain input from the team leader. Although input from peers can be used, it too can have its painful drawbacks and should be considered accordingly.

Yearly feedback on performance should not be the goal of the appraisal system. Rather, a system for frequent feedback should be in place. The performance appraisal can then be a summary of this ongoing feedback process and a time for agreement on goals and objectives as well as a report on progress toward meeting the previously set goals and objectives.

2. *A system for determining salary increases.* A performance appraisal process that includes this feature is focused on competition. Each staff member competes with the others for the higher positions in order to gain personal compensation. This system forces the supervisors to rank staff members. Not only is that difficult to do, but value judgments over which position is more important cloud the supervisors' perception of staff members' actual performance. Eliminate this as a feature of the evaluation process. Establish just compensation and pay accordingly.

The Navy of many years ago believed in the "bell curve" distribution of personal performance. Evaluations of groups were required to distribute the marks so that there were the correct number of exceptional performers, average performers, and poor performers. Naturally, each person discussed their marks with others. The system was demotivating to almost everyone. It wasn't used to determine salary but was used to determine position for promotion. Today we know better

than to expect a standard distribution of performance levels in every group.

3. *A formal system of communication between the staff member or volunteer and the evaluator.* While the appraisal can be a time to document a formal meeting between the employee and evaluator, there should be frequent meetings of this nature throughout the year. Because people desire to know how their supervisors view their work, the supervisor should note immediately when a worker's performance is not meeting the expectations or goals they have agreed upon.

If an annual performance appraisal is conducted with paid staff members and team leaders who work with the staff, it should include at least four elements:

1. *An opportunity for the staff member or team leader to evaluate his or her own performance.* This provides the church worker a chance to review the goals and objectives previously set and identify reasons they have or have not been met. It allows the staff members and team leaders to celebrate the successes of the past year (most congregations do not take enough time to celebrate past successes) and to identify areas of personal achievement the supervisor might have overlooked. It provides an opportunity to identify areas where increased training could be beneficial.

> **I say to everyone among you not to think of yourself more highly than you ought to think, but to think with sober judgment, each according to the measure of faith that God has assigned.**
>
> —*Romans 12:3*

✔ **2.** *Goal setting by the staff member or team leader.* As noted before, people accept and strive to meet goals they have helped set. The appraisal should give the church worker the opportunity to review past goals and to set new ones.

✔ **3.** *Discussion of barriers and obstacles.* Allow discussion of barriers or roadblocks or resources missing which could explain apparent failures.

✔ **4.** *Joint discussion between the church worker and the supervisor.* The church worker's evaluation is returned to the supervisor, who carefully reads it, adds his or her own comments, and reviews the entire process with the worker. Together they review the past evaluation period and establish goals and objectives for the following year. They discuss the barriers, resources, and obstacles they have identified and work together to remove them.

Performance appraisals conducted in this manner provide encouragement and recognition for past achievements. Staff members and volunteers are not competing. There is no ranking about which they can discuss and feel dishonored. The process provides and encourages open communication. This system can recognize exceptional performance.

Use the following questions to evaluate your current performance appraisal process.

How often do you communicate directly with your staff members and key volunteers concerning their performance?

annually / semiannualy / quarterly / monthly / whenever necessary

How often would you like to communicate with them about their performance? _____

Do you participate with your staff members or key volunteers in the establishment of goals and objectives?

never / occasionally / sometimes / frequently / whenever necessary

What would you like to do? _____

Do you help your employees and key volunteers to identify barriers or obstacles to their accomplishment of goals or objectives?

never / occasionally / sometimes / frequently / whenever necessary

What would you like to do? _____

Used correctly, the performance appraisal process becomes a positive motivator and a true recognition system for the staff members and volunteers. Believing that one's true performance is being observed and honestly evaluated is positive motivation. Sometimes, it is all the reward a church worker needs to continue to excel.

An example of a performance appraisal is included on the next few pages. Find ways to improve this system for your use. Consider how it might be used to recognize exceptional performance by volunteers as well as staff members.

[YOUR CHURCH'S NAME]

PERSONNEL DEVELOPMENT REVIEW

Year: 199_

Confidential: Employee Input

Date: _____

Employee: _____

As workers together in God's kingdom and at this church, all of us seek to use our gifts, talents, and abilities to follow God's call in our lives. We all seek to do the highest quality job we can do in God's service. This means that we must work together as well as individually to accomplish God's mission for our church.

This part of the evaluation allows you to provide input. Please complete this process as honestly and completely as possible.

I. Activities

1. Consider your job description. How does this relate to what you actually do?

2. What parts of your work require the most time?

3. What parts of your work do you feel are the most important?

4. What parts (if any) of your work do you feel are unnecessary?

5. What parts (if any) of your work do you feel could best be done by someone else?

6. What responsibilities do others have that you feel you are best-suited to accomplish?

7. Are you sufficiently trained to do your best in all areas? If not, what additional training is required?

8. Are there barriers or obstacles that prevent you from doing your best? If so, what are they, and how can they be removed?

9. Do you feel that your personal gifts and personality are being utilized in the best way? If not, what should be done?

10. Identify specific aspects of your responsibilities you wish to discuss with your supervisor.

II. Future Ministry Goals and Objectives

1. Identify your ministry goals and objectives for the coming year. Be as specific as possible.

2. Identify your action plans to accomplish these goals and objectives. Identify the specific results you expect.

3. What specific additional resources will you require in order to achieve these goals and objectives?

III. Current Ministry Goals and Objectives

Review your ministry goals and objectives for the current year. Identify and explain your progress toward these goals and objectives.

IV. PERSONAL QUALITY

For each of the statements below, indicate whether you strongly agree (SA), agree (A), are neutral (N), disagree (D), or strongly disagree (SD). Provide an honest appraisal of yourself.

Attribute	SA	A	N	D	SD
I am a cooperative team player.					
I seek the highest quality in my work.					
I seek to meet the expectations of all my "customers."					
I take responsibility for my own actions.					
I strongly support our church's mission.					
I am a hard worker.					
I am honest and loyal.					
I have a positive attitude.					
I enjoy working at our church.					

V. Personal Goals and Objectives

1. Identify your personal goals and objectives for the coming year. Be as specific as possible and include target dates for completion.

2. Identify what training or additional resources you will need in order to achieve these goals.

TEAM MINISTRY
CHAPTER • SEVEN

[YOUR CHURCH'S NAME]
PERSONNEL DEVELOPMENT REVIEW
YEAR : 1 9 9 _

Confidential: Employee/Supervisor Interaction

Date: _____

Employee: _____

Job title: _____

Supervisor: _____

Length of time in this position: _____

This annual development review has two parts. The first is your evaluation of yourself and your performance. The second is this personal interaction with your supervisor. These reviews are intended to help you provide the highest quality work for the ministry of our church.

I. Employee Input

First, let's review the input you have provided.
(You may write additional comments on the employee's input form.)

II. Additional Comments

A. Balance

A person's feelings about himself or herself encompass several aspects—physical, spiritual, emotional, and mental. A person's priorities might include his or her attention to God, work, self, and family. Keeping these feelings and priorities in proper balance is important. How do you evaluate your overall balance during the past year?

Exceptional ___   Excellent ___   Good ___   Fair ___   Poor ___

Comments:

B. General Comments

Use this time to discuss specific needs, accomplishments, difficulties, opportunities, attitudes, salary needs, general working environment, peer comments, or other topics.

III. Acknowledgment

I have read this evaluation and have had an opportunity to discuss it with my supervisor.

_____   _____
(Signature of employee)   (Date)

_____   _____
(Signature of supervisor)   (Date)

INTRINSIC MOTIVATION

Another positive motivator for church staff will occur when you help your staff and volunteer group to take pride in their service. Whether paid or unpaid, each church worker should recognize his or her role in serving the Body of Christ. The church worker's labor is more than a job. While each should expect fair compensation for his or her labor, it is likely that a church worker receives lower compensation than he or she might receive for doing the same work at another organization or business. In addition, the congregational ministry team is working in a role of serving the Body of Christ.

There is reward in serving the Body of Christ and in serving *in* the Body of Christ.

> **Whatever your task, put yourselves into it, as done for the Lord and not for your masters, since you know that from the Lord you will receive the inheritance as your reward; you serve the Lord Christ.**
> —*Colossians 3:23-24*

While Colossians 3:23-24 obviously exhorts people in all occupations and employment to recognize their service to Jesus, for those in the church it has a double reward.

> **[Saul said to David,] "May the LORD reward you with good for what you have done to me this day."**
> —*1 Samuel 24:19b*

Work in the service of the Lord Jesus should be an act of humble servanthood but not an act of enslavement. One who approaches his or her work in the congregation from the perspective of servitude will serve out of *obligation* rather than *obedience*.

> **Tend the flock of God that is in your charge, exercising the oversight, not under compulsion but willingly, as God would have you do it—not for sordid gain but eagerly.**
> —*1 Peter 5:2*

Service for the slave is narrow-minded, not so much on the part of the slave but more on the part of the slave driver. Slaves follow orders and prop up the honor of their masters; servants recognize their giftedness, which is given by God. Slaves see the *job*; servants see the *calling*. Slaves seek the *credit* for their efforts; servants *honor* God with their efforts. Slaves see people as *interruptions* to their work; servants see people as the *reason* for their work.

> " 'Truly I tell you, just as you did it to one of the least of these who are members of my family, you did it to me.' "
> —*Matthew 25:40*

According to *Merriam Webster's Collegiate Dictionary*, tenth edition, to serve means "to be of use . . . to be favorable, opportune, or convenient . . . to furnish or supply with something needed or desired . . . to answer the needs of." Isn't this personally motivating? Do you believe people desire to be of use?

Help your staff and volunteers to recognize their service in the Lord's work. They will receive personal satisfaction and fulfillment in recognition of this honor.

A POSITIVE WORK ENVIRONMENT

You have worked hard to establish a working environment that is supportive of an empowered staff and volunteer team. Do you know just how great it is to be able to work in such an environment? For those who have worked in positions outside the church, even for companies that strive for quality, a positive, Christian environment will be refreshing. Nearly any person called of God will enjoy working in your environment. That, too, is a reward!

Not all church work is fun. Not all church work is satisfying. People do burn out in church work. However, the steps you have taken will help to reduce and remove the negative motivators. It will resolve the conflict. It will create an environment where the work of the Holy Spirit is obvious. That is great motivation!

FAIR COMPENSATION

Setting fair compensation standards was previously discussed. Money is rarely a positive motivator for doing God's work. Although raises or bonuses are great to receive, the spending habits of people in an affluent culture quickly consume any salary increase. We each struggle with economic tension. Consequently, a raise or bonus is quickly forgotten. The impression that remains, however, is the fact of the raise or bonus.

Within the limited resources of the congregation, plan hiring, purchasing resources, and training in such a way that a position can be secure and that some amount of pay raise will be possible.

Money has the potential of being a highly negative motivator, especially if the compensation varies widely among staff members in a congregation or among the leaders in a denominational system. As much as you might desire to keep salaries and wages confidential, people will share information about their compensation with one another. This guarantees at least one of the participants will be unhappy, unless the compensation system is carefully researched, set, and implemented. Use available resources to set compensation ranges for employees. Set compensation for new employees within the ranges already established. For example, if you set a salary range of $14,000 to $18,000 for full-time administrative assistants, make sure this is the range for all full-time administrative assistants, including new hires.

Congregations often find themselves in situations in which the needs of the ministry increase but the financial resources do not. Even though your staff members may accept additional work, try to help restructure their priorities. When staff members acquire more work, either increase their compensation for the additional work, reduce their responsibilities in other areas, or provide them with additional help to accomplish both the old and the new work. This kind of rebalancing of work priorities is hard to understand for highly ambitious church leaders who have succeeded by adding more and more work to their own plates. But be cautious of the moral and physical collapse that results from a failure to know one's own limits and the limits of others.

The laborer deserves to be paid.
—Luke 10:7

RECOGNITION

There is an old saying: "Praise in public, correct in private."

Whether or not people desire praise for their individual efforts, it is important to recognize their contributions publicly. Be creative in ways that can help this happen. Some people, out of deep humility, do not want any recognition or credit for what they do. It is important for others, however, to see the contributions of such people recognized and appreciated.

Let another praise you, and not your own mouth—a stranger, and not your own lips.
—Proverbs 27:2

A modern-day management method has been labeled "Management by Wandering Around." The essence of this style is that the manager can determine the true nature of the work by being where the workers are working. One of the best attributes of this management style is the opportunity to "catch" someone doing something *right*! This gives you the opportunity to praise the person publicly and instantly as you see this performance. Not only does this praise encourage positive performance, but the person is honored in front of others. In addition, those who hear will also see an example of positive performance and its recognition.

Public recognition of exceptional performance

can occur on several levels. Exceptional performance may be recognized at a workstation, in front of the staff and volunteers at a meeting, in front of the governing board, at a church banquet, on the front page of your newsletter, or in front of the congregation at worship. You may desire to establish a system that determines which performance is recognized at which event. Although the intent is not to create a competitive system, recognizing someone in front of the congregation may be the highest honor and might not be the appropriate way to recognize all types of exceptional performance.

[Jesus said,] "He may say to you, 'Friend, move up higher'; then you will be honored in the presence of all who sit at the table with you."

—Luke 14:10b

At each of their weekly meetings of the entire staff, one church has a time for "The Winners of the Week." This is a time for individual staff members to recognize the positive performance of other staff members. A children's ministry team leader might recognize the exceptional help provided by a maintenance person. The youth team leader may recognize the exceptional help provided by mailing team in completing a mailing. The singles' director may recognize the help provided by the financial assistant in budgeting. Frequently, when one person is recognized, that individual then passes the honor to another in

recognition of his or her support. In this way, each is honored in front of the entire staff.

Many congregations have established an annual volunteer banquet. All persons who have volunteered in ministry during the year are invited. At some churches the staff serves the meal to the volunteers. This is another public recognition of service.

After a major event that has taken an exceptional amount of effort and energy from certain staff members and volunteers, recognize their effort by holding a special fun day or party. Take the team to see a movie or go bowling or play miniature golf. Not only will this be a fun way to recognize the team's effort and "officially" recognize a time of relaxation, but also it will provide a time to build positive relationships.

PRIVATE RECOGNITION

Not all recognition needs to be public. At times a simple thank-you note to someone brings joy. A birthday card or anniversary card to volunteers lets them know that they are special. While it may not be possible to send birthday cards to all members of the congregation, individual directors at some churches send birthday cards to their key volunteers.

When you catch someone doing something right, you can praise that person even if no one else hears. During the course of one-on-one meetings with individuals you can take time to recognize and reinforce a positive behavior or performance.

PROMOTIONS

A promotion to a new level of responsibility is another way to recognize exceptional performance. It is not as easy in a congregation as it might be in a corporation, due to the smaller size of the staff. However, when an opportunity arises to create a new position, consider moving an existing staff member to fill the new vacancy. In addition to creating the promotion, you will also provide some cross-training.

Filling vacant positions on a compensated staff with existing committed members of the congregation may also be viewed as promotion. Selecting faithful volunteers to perform in compensated roles shows your staff and key volunteers that promotions do occur.

Honestly evaluate your recognition and reward systems. Do you encourage exceptional performance? Do you recognize the efforts of those whose labor may not be as visible as that of others? Do you provide opportunities for your employees and key volunteers to recognize publicly the efforts of others who support them? Think of simple ways to improve the recognition and reward system for those who labor with you. Write down your ideas here.

A HEART FOR GOD

During a conference for church leaders in Omaha, Nebraska, key pastors and leaders came together looking for ways to develop stronger, healthier ministries. The opening speaker knew the importance of tapping into each listener's imaginative and creative potential early in the day; he began his speech by saying, "The Nebraska Cornhuskers football team is one of the winningest teams in the world. This team has captured the hearts of tens of thousands of raving fans. What would it take to put a winning team like the Cornhuskers together in every congregation? Imagine the world getting as excited and interested in following Jesus Christ as they are in following Nebraska football!"

Tom Osborne, the head coach of this championship team understands the importance of high quality recruiting, training, motivating, and implementing. A winning team doesn't happen accidentally. It happens intentionally! If you are to be intentional about team ministry, you will be driven by conviction, commitment, and courage.

The process of building a quality, winning team should be developed from the inside out. This is called conviction. Out of the heart come values, vision, and vitality. That's why

having a heart for God is a prerequisite for creating anything of quality. God is the initiator of and the one who completes our achievements, in which we offer our best efforts for God. God is also the instigator and sustainer of healthy functional relationships. We are convicted by God to do our best.

Following upon conviction is commitment. Building a high-quality championship ministry team is a lot of hard work. When winners emerge it isn't simply luck. One of the authors visited with the owner of Anthony's Pier Four in Boston. The restaurant is world famous for its exceptional food. The owner was perched beside the host stand and was asked, "How did this establishment become so successful?" Without hesitation the owner said, "Some people say it's luck. However, I've discovered that the harder I work, the luckier I get." Luck is haphazard, random success, which comes from merely imitating cultural fads and trends. The kind of lasting success required for a dynamic ministry requires commitment to excellence. That kind of human commitment is expressed by

the motto, "Whatever it takes!" But God demonstrated an even more extravagant commitment when Jesus Christ was born to live, die, and rise again so that all might experience God's love—today, tomorrow, and forever.

After conviction and commitment comes courage. Courageous action results in building confident championship teams. Jesus' call is the difficult way. It is not the way that the world would choose. Jesus said, "If any want to become my followers, let them deny themselves and take up their cross and follow me" (Matt. 16:24). A quality ministry team is not managed and maintained through the paths of least resistance. The easy way is usually not the best way. There are often tough decisions that must be made.

During a particularly difficult time in our ministry a friend advised, "God is more concerned about our character than about our comfort." It was a character-building time for the whole ministry team. The path of least resistance was tempting. However, the courageous action was to do the right thing and not the easiest thing.

As you build your winning team, may God give you the wisdom and the will to be the champion God dreamed of when you and your ministry were created.

A SPIRITUAL GIFTS SURVEY

Now there are
varieties of gifts,
but the same Spirit,
and there are varieties
of services,
but the same Lord;
and there are varieties
of activities,
but it is the same God
who activates all of
them in everyone.
To each is given the
manifestation of the Spirit
for the common good.

1 Corinthians 12:4-7

INSTRUCTIONS

Using the rating sheet on page 117, rate each of the following statements according to the degree of satisfaction you have had or anticipate you would have in performing the task described. There are no right or wrong answers. Please answer as honestly and sincerely as possible.

0 = no satisfaction   1 = a little satisfaction
2 = some satisfaction   3 = much satisfaction

When are you finished, follow the instructions at the bottom of the rating sheet.

1. Looking for opportunities to help others in their task.
2. Concentrating on practical things rather than on the theory behind them.
3. Gaining understanding of persons with special needs.
4. Assimilating information from several sources to find the answer to a question.
5. Giving practical solutions to problems facing the church.
6. Trusting God to do what he promises in Scripture.
7. Patiently listening to people who are discouraged rather than directing them to someone else.
8. Feeling joyfully confident in sharing the reality of the living Christ.
9. Having responsibility for the spiritual care of a group of children, youth, or adults.
10. Seeking out Christian projects that need money rather than waiting for appeals for funds.
11. Distinguishing between a work that is centered in Christ and a counterfeit without doing a lot of research.
12. Serving as chairman of a committee.
13. Giving direction to people under your supervision and making decisions that affect them.
14. Bringing about changes in attitude, values, or conduct through the communication of biblical truths.
15. Sensing conditions that are not pleasing to God and speaking boldly to correct them.
16. Being used of God to transform lives physically, emotionally, or spiritually.
17. Serving Christ among people of another culture.
18. Being accepted as a spiritual authority among churches.
19. Helping the church by using your creative or regular work skills.
20. Joyfully praying for others on a regular basis.

21. Entertaining guests in your home as a ministry.
22. Serving in the church to greet members and visitors, making them feel glad they came.
23. Privately speaking to God in an unknown language.
24. Using your musical ability to minister in the worship service of your church.
25. Performing support tasks that free Christian leaders to do things that they do best.
26. Doing things with your hands rather than talking to a person with a problem.
27. Cheerfully visiting those in hospitals, prison, or rest homes.
28. Reading the Bible and other books regularly to gain knowledge.
29. Applying biblical principles to help others in problem situations.
30. Being assured by the Lord that he will do a seemingly impossible task for the furtherance of his work.
31. Maintaining a belief in a person in the midst of repeated failures or giving time to someone whom others have given up on.
32. Talking with others about your experience of trusting Christ as Savior and Lord.
33. Following up on a wayward or neglected member of the church.
34. Earning money with the purpose of supporting Christian work.
35. Detecting whether a person is genuine in his or her witness and having courage to discuss it with him or her.
36. Guiding a group in formulating its goals and purposes.
37. Planning out the details in order to guide a group in its work.
38. Guiding believers in a patient, positive, and loving way through sharing the Scripture.
39. Sensing that others are persuaded of the rightness of the message you proclaim.
40. Praying for the sick and finding some positive results.
41. Easily understanding the manners and customs of people from a different culture.
42. Preparing strategies for the establishment of new churches.
43. Making needed furniture or equipment for the Lord's work.
44. Frequently finding positive results from prayer.
45. Using your home for get-acquainted potlucks for new people.
46. Spotting church visitors and being a conversation starter.
47. Receiving a message rom God and sharing it with others in an unlearned language.
48. Writing, arranging, or training others in music so that Christ's work is enhanced.
49. Doing routine tasks that help to carry out a ministry.
50. Being known as reliable and punctual in getting a task done.
51. Working with physical or emotional problems to alleviate suffering.
52. Gaining understanding of difficult passages of Scripture.
53. Indicating what should be done rather than why it should be done.
54. Trusting God enough to sacrifice and work hard to accomplish a seemingly impossible task.
55. Giving encouragement to someone who has done a good job.
56. Reaching out to the unchurched rather than working with the growth and equipping of believers.
57. Praying for specific needs of people who look to you for care.
58. Giving sacrificially and joyfully for the work of the Lord in the confidence that God will meet your needs.
59. Quickly sensing a person's motivation.
60. Generating excitement among others about the

goals of the church.

61. Monitoring the progress of a program for quality and cost.

62. Devoting a large amount of time to study of the Bible and related resources.

63. Sensing urgency to share a message from God regarding a current social problem.

64. Being used of God to successfully deal with problems that are beyond human ability.

65. Adapting easily to life in a different culture.

66. Being called on by churches to give counsel for their problems.

67. Making clothing or other items to provide for the needy at home or abroad.

68. Discovering that prayer is a fulfilling and rewarding experience.

69. Using your home for a neighborhood Bible study.

70. Serving as an usher or traffic guide to help people in and out of church gatherings.

71. Interpreting the speech of one who speaks in tongues.

72. Being used of God to sing a message that edifies the people.

73. Doing tasks that are supportive to others in leadership rather than being a leader of others.

74. Applying available resources to get a task done.

75. Assisting people who are disabled.

76. Sharing insight from study that will help the Christian cause.

77. Intuitively sensing direction in the midst of a complicated issue.

78. Knowing God's specific will for the future growth of his work even when others have been uncertain.

79. Bringing help to those who are guilty, perplexed, depressed, afflicted, or wavering.

80. Knowing that others have come to a personal relationship with Jesus Christ through your-sharing of the gospel message.

81. Spending time with a group or an individual in order to build relationships.

82. Giving without thought of recognition or the response of the recipient.

83. Being asked for your evaluation of whether something is genuine or false.

84. Motivating others to get involved in the Lord's work.

85. Guiding and directing others to meaningfully involve them in church.

86. Giving time to discovering resources and preparing aids that will be useful in communicating the biblical truth.

87. Feeling strongly that God has given you a special message to share that edifies, warns, or rebukes others.

88. Being used of God to deliver a person from domination by an evil spirit.

89. Learning a foreign language in order to effectively communicate the gospel.

90. Finding others willing to follow your counsel on spiritual matters.

91. Being asked to use your creative, decorative, or artistic skills for Christ's work.

92. Being drawn to prayer frequently each day for significant periods of time.

93. Finding that getting your home ready for guests is a pleasure.

94. Being a "climate setter" by making the church a warm, friendly place.

95. Recognizing that unknown tongues, when spoken in public, need an interpretation.

96. Bringing a spirit of praise through music in the worship of God.

97. Being asked to do a specific routine task to help another person.

98. Working behind the scenes to facilitate the work to the church.

99. Loving and abiding the seemingly unlovable.

100. Sorting out the significant from the secondary

facts on a issue.

101. Discovering practical ways of applying biblical truths to life.

102. Finding excitement rather than discouragement in extremely difficult challenges.

103. Challenging the complacent and redirecting the wayward.

104. Being sensitive to the feelings, needs, and desires of a non-Christian.

105. Staying with a group for a year or more to provide guidance and continuity.

106. Viewing giving as an investment in the kingdom of God with an exciting anticipation of the spiritual returns.

107. Giving reliable evaluation as to whether a teaching is of God, of Satan, or of human origin.

108. Understanding a vision of how the church can move forward in its ministry.

109. Organizing the efforts of a group in order to help it reach its goal.

110. Working through the complexities of a passage of Scripture so that its truth can be shared in a clear and concise way.

111. Telling others what God has revealed to you regarding future or present events.

112. Feeling strongly directed to pray for some acute needs.

113. Using your professional skills to help deprived people in another culture.

114. Gathering a new group of converts to form a new church.

115. Using your skills to maintain and beautify the church property or grounds.

116. Believing deeply that God releases his power in response to your prayer.

117. Discovering the joy of sharing life with guests around your dining room table.

118. Giving information about various ministries of the church to newcomers.

119. Desiring to praise God through the use of tongues.

120. Being available to train your musical gifts for use in the Lord's work.

RATING SHEET

Rating Scale:
0 = no satisfaction   1 = a little satisfaction
2 = some satisfaction   3 = much satisfaction

DESCRIPTIONS OF THE SPIRITUAL GIFTS

A. **Helping** — The gift of helping is the special ability that God gives to certain members of the Body of Christ to invest the talents they have in the life and ministry of other members of the Body, enabling those others to increase the effectiveness of their own spiritual gifts.

B. **Service** — The gift of service is the special ability that God gives to certain members of the Body of Christ to identify the unmet needs involved in a task related to God's work, and to make use of available resources to meet those needs and help accomplish the desired results.

C. **Mercy** — The gift of mercy is the special ability that God gives to certain members of the Body of Christ to feel genuine empathy and compassion for individuals (both Christian and non-Christian) who suffer distressing physical,

					TOTAL	GIFT
1 0 1 2 3	25 0 1 2 3	49 0 1 2 3	73 0 1 2 3	97 0 1 2 3	A	
2 0 1 2 3	26 0 1 2 3	50 0 1 2 3	74 0 1 2 3	98 0 1 2 3	B	
3 0 1 2 3	27 0 1 2 3	51 0 1 2 3	75 0 1 2 3	99 0 1 2 3	C	
4 0 1 2 3	28 0 1 2 3	52 0 1 2 3	76 0 1 2 3	100 0 1 2 3	D	
5 0 1 2 3	29 0 1 2 3	53 0 1 2 3	77 0 1 2 3	101 0 1 2 3	E	
6 0 1 2 3	30 0 1 2 3	54 0 1 2 3	78 0 1 2 3	102 0 1 2 3	F	
7 0 1 2 3	31 0 1 2 3	55 0 1 2 3	79 0 1 2 3	103 0 1 2 3	G	
8 0 1 2 3	32 0 1 2 3	56 0 1 2 3	80 0 1 2 3	104 0 1 2 3	H	
9 0 1 2 3	33 0 1 2 3	57 0 1 2 3	81 0 1 2 3	105 0 1 2 3	I	
10 0 1 2 3	34 0 1 2 3	58 0 1 2 3	82 0 1 2 3	106 0 1 2 3	J	
11 0 1 2 3	35 0 1 2 3	59 0 1 2 3	83 0 1 2 3	107 0 1 2 3	K	
12 0 1 2 3	36 0 1 2 3	60 0 1 2 3	84 0 1 2 3	108 0 1 2 3	L	
13 0 1 2 3	37 0 1 2 3	61 0 1 2 3	85 0 1 2 3	109 0 1 2 3	M	
14 0 1 2 3	38 0 1 2 3	62 0 1 2 3	86 0 1 2 3	113 0 1 2 3	N	
15 0 1 2 3	39 0 1 2 3	63 0 1 2 3	87 0 1 2 3	111 0 1 2 3	O	
16 0 1 2 3	40 0 1 2 3	64 0 1 2 3	88 0 1 2 3	112 0 1 2 3	P	
17 0 1 2 3	41 0 1 2 3	65 0 1 2 3	89 0 1 2 3	11 0 1 2 3	Q	
18 0 1 2 3	42 0 1 2 3	66 0 1 2 3	90 0 1 2 3	114 0 1 2 3	R	
19 0 1 2 3	43 0 1 2 3	67 0 1 2 3	91 0 1 2 3	115 0 1 2 3	S	
20 0 1 2 3	44 0 1 2 3	68 0 1 2 3	92 0 1 2 3	116 0 1 2 3	T	
21 0 1 2 3	45 0 1 2 3	69 0 1 2 3	93 0 1 2 3	117 0 1 2 3	U	
22 0 1 2 3	46 0 1 2 3	70 0 1 2 3	94 0 1 2 3	118 0 1 2 3	V	
23 0 1 2 3	47 0 1 2 3	71 0 1 2 3	95 0 1 2 3	119 0 1 2 3	W	
24 0 1 2 3	48 0 1 2 3	72 0 1 2 3	96 0 1 2 3	120 0 1 2 3	X	

Add the responses for each line, A through X, and write the sum in the "Total" column. Using the key, find the names of those three gifts, and write the names on the appropriate lines in the "Gift" column. These may be your primary spiritual gifts. Turn to the descriptions of the spiritual gifts and read about your gifts, keeping in mind that this survey is a tool to help you begin thinking about your spiritual gifts—not the final word on your gifts.

A. Helping
B. Service
C. Mercy
D. Knowledge
E. Wisdom
F. Faith
G. Exhortation
H. Evangelism
I. Pastoring
J. Giving
K. Discernment
L. Leadership
M. Administration
N. Teaching
O. Prophecy
P. Healing and miracles
Q. Missions
R. Apostleship
S. Craftsmanship
T. Intercession
U. Hospitality (home)
V. Hospitality (church)
W. Tongues and intepretation
X. Music

mental, or emotional problems, and to translate that compassion into cheerfully done deeds that reflect Christ's love and alleviate the suffering.

D. Knowledge — The gift of knowledge is the special ability that God gives to certain members of the Body of Christ to discover, accumulate, analyze, and clarify information and ideas that are pertinent to the well-being of the Body.

E. Wisdom — The gift of wisdom is the special ability that God gives to certain members of the Body of Christ to know the mind of the Holy Spirit in such a way as to receive insight into how given knowledge may best be applied to specific needs arising in the Body of Christ.

F. Faith — The gift of faith is the special ability that God gives to certain members of the Body of Christ to discern with extraordinary confidence the will and purposes of God for his work.

G. Exhortation — The gift of exhortation is the special ability that God gives to certain members of the Body of Christ to share words of comfort, consolation, encouragement, and counsel with other members of the Body in such a way that they feel helped and healed.

H. Evangelism — The gift of evangelism is the special ability that God gives to certain members of the Body of Christ to share the gospel with unbelievers in such a way that men and women become disciples of Jesus and responsible members of the Body of Christ.

I. Pastoring — The gift of pastoring is the special ability that God gives to certain members of the Body of Christ to assume a long-term personal responsibility for the spiritual welfare of a group of believers.

J. Giving — The gift of giving is the special ability that God gives to certain members of the Body of Christ to cheerfully contribute their material resources to the work of the Lord.

K. Discernment — The gift of discernment is the special ability that God gives to certain members of the Body of Christ to know with assurance whether certain behavior purported to be of God is in reality divine, human, or satanic.

L. Leadership — The gift of leadership is the special ability that God gives to certain members of the Body of Christ to set goals in accordance with God's purpose for the future and to communicate these goals to others in such a way that they voluntarily and harmoniously work together to accomplish those goals for the glory of God.

M. Administration — The gift of administration is the special ability that God gives to certain members of the Body of Christ to understand clearly the immediate and long-range goals of a particular unit of the Body of Christ and to devise and execute effective plans for the accomplishment of those goals.

N. Teaching — The gift of teaching is the special ability that God gives to certain members of the Body of Christ to communicate information relevant to the health and ministry of the Body and its members in such a way that others will learn.

O. Prophecy — The gift of prophecy is the special ability that God gives to certain members of the Body of Christ to receive and communicate an immediate message of God to his people through a divinely anointed utterance.

P. **Healing and miracles** — The gift of healing and miracles is the special ability that God gives to certain members of the Body of Christ to serve as human intermediaries through whom it pleases God to cure illness and restore health apart from the use of natural means.

Q. **Missions** — The gift of missions is the special ability that God gives to certain members of the Body of Christ to share whatever other spiritual gifts they have in another culture.

R. **Apostleship** — The gift of apostleship is the special ability that God gives to certain members of the Body of Christ to serve as human intermediaries through whom it pleases God to perform powerful acts that are perceived by observers to have altered the ordinary course of nature.

S. **Craftsmanship** — The gift of craftsmanship is the special ability that God gives to certain members of the Body of Christ to fix, restore, maintain, and operate equipment, tools, and machinery.

T. **Intercession**— The gift of intercession is the special ability that God gives to certain members of the Body of Christ to pray for extended periods of time on a regular basis and see frequent and specific answers to their prayers, to a degree much greater than that expected of the average Christian.

U. **Hospitality (home)** — The gift of hospitality at home is the special ability that God gives

to certain members of the Body of Christ to provide an open house and a warm welcome to those in need of food and lodging.

V. **Hospitality (church)** — The gift of hospitality at church is the special ability that God gives to certain members of the Body of Christ to provide a warm welcome to those who come to worship.

W. **Tongues and interpretation** — The gift of tongues is the special ability that God gives to certain members of the Body of Christ to speak to God in a language they have never learned or to receive and communicate an immediate message of God to his people through a divinely anointed utterance in a language they have never learned.

The gift of interpretation is the special ability that God gives to certain members of the Body of Christ to make known in the vernacular the message of one who speaks in tongues.

X. **Music** — The gift of music is the special ability that God gives to certain members of the Body of Christ to entertain, perform, act, dance, and speak in front of others to enhance worship.

Nazarene Theological College

B10775

TRAINING INSTITUTES AND SEMINARS

The Robert H. Schuller Institute for Successful Church Leadership, 12141 Lewis Street, Garden Grove, CA 92640

Seminars held yearly on the campus of the Crystal Cathedral are inspirational and practical. Thousands of pastors and lay leaders have been renewed in hope and vision through Schuller's institute.

Church Growth, Inc., 1921 South Myrtle Avenue, Monrovia, CA 91016 (818-305-1280)

Win Arn and Charles Arn have been the leaders in preparing hands-on, practical products for helping churches implement church growth principles. They also offer helpful seminars.

The Charles E. Fuller Institute of Evangelism and Church Growth, P.O. Box 91990, Pasadena, CA 91101

This institute is on the leading edge of the church growth movement. Many seminars are offered year-round, both on the Fuller campus and around the country. Fuller Theological Seminary offers a doctor of ministry degree in church growth.

Willow Creek Community Church, 67 E. Algonquin Road, South Barrington, IL 60010

Pastored by Bill Hybels, this is the leading-edge church for boomers. Using highly presentational worship each weekend, they reach thousands of unchurched boomers. They hold conferences each year.

Saddleback Valley Community Church, 23456 Madero, Suite 100, Mission Viejo, CA 92691

Pastored by Rick Warren, this boomer church uses participational worship each weekend. Started by Warren over eleven years ago, the church has an average attendence in worship of over four thousand and has only recently settled into a permanent structure. Conferences are held each year.

Community Church of Joy Leadership Center, 16635 N. 51st Avenue, Glendale, AZ 85306 (602-938-1460, ext. 134)

Each year, beginning on the evening of the second Monday after Easter, Community Church of Joy offers a four-day conference on "Effective Evangelism for Mainline Congregations." The conference offers fresh insights on how to penetrate the culture with the good news of Christ. An East-Coast conference is held every August.

Church Growth Center, P.O. Box 145, Corunna, IN 46730 (800-626-8515)

Directed by Dr. Kent Hunter, a Lutheran Church, Missouri Synod pastor, the Church Growth center offers resources and seminars on church growth from a Lutheran perspective.